JASPER JOHNS

GEORGES BOUDAILLE

JASPER JOHNS

RIZZOLI
NEW YORK

First published in the United States of America in 1989 by

RIZZOLI INTERNATIONAL PUBLICATIONS, INC.
300 Park Avenue South, New York, NY 10010

© *1989 Ediciones Polígrafa, S. A.*
Translated by Asti Hustvedt
Reproduction rights: Jasper Johns / VAGA New York

LC 89-42926
ISBN 0-8478-1143-3

Printed and bound in Spain by La Polígrafa, S. A.
Parets del Vallès (Barcelona)
Dep. Leg. B. 21.940 - 1989

CONTENTS

Who is Jasper Johns?

Is there anyone who does not know about Jasper Johns' *Flags, Targets, Numbers* or *Letters*? For an artist of his stature, such a view is at best perfunctory since it takes into account only the most popular aspects of his work, and moreover, only the work from his early period, completed when he was between twenty-five and thirty years old.

Today his art is universally recognized and Johns has attained the prestige that puts him side by side with the greatest artists of the century, with Picasso, Léger or Miró.

Yet outside of his own country, the full breadth and diversity of his work is unknown. As for the man, he guards his privacy, choosing to remain elusive and mysterious.

Strangely enough, while the press has unanimously praised his work, there have been few monographs published outside of the United States.

Here then is an artist, who at the age of twenty-four (any earlier work was destroyed) had already found his major themes, themes he has continued to use throughout his long career, and continues to use today.

He has remained faithful to certain principles all along: his claim that "things have no intrinsic value"; his dislike of drawing; and his use of uncomplicated themes borrowed from the public domain, such as the American flag, targets, numbers, letters, and later on, plaster casts of parts of the body.

Johns was one of the first artists to incorporate objects into his paintings, and while influenced by Marcel Duchamp, he differs from the French artist in that he does not use these objects by themselves, with the exception of a few plaster casts, but integrates them into his paintings. And finally, he played an important, if unconscious, role in going beyond Abstract Expressionism. Action Painting was not enough for him and he can be considered one of the initiators of Pop Art as well.

Marcelin Pleynet,[1] who has closely followed American art for many years, claims that "Johns' art is distinguished from that of his contemporaries in that it both integrates and goes beyond Abstract Expressionism." A crucial issue that has been debated at length is whether or not he should be included in the American Pop Art movement.

Lucy Lippard, another astute observer of the American scene and a historian of Pop Art insists that, according to certain definite criteria, only five artists, all from New York, can properly be labelled as Pop: Andy Warhol, Roy Lichtenstein, Tom Wesselman, James Rosenquist and Claes Oldenburg. However, she goes on to say that the work of Jasper Johns provided the true point of departure for Pop Art. And while his sense of pictorial irony is related to that of Duchamp, he is, like most American painters, first and foremost a painter, ideology taking second place.[2]

Not having followed Jasper Johns' career from the beginning, and not being an inside observer any more than a confidant, my intentions in this monologue are not to present new, never before published information, nor are they to revolutionize the critical approach to his work, but, much more modestly, to examine it from the perspective of a European art historian. The work of Jasper Johns, once it is stripped of its many playful references and visual puns — which, more than anything, have served to make it noticed rather than really known — and of its disruptive character within an artistic context still dominated by Abstract Expressionism and its direct descendant, Color field Painting, rightfully belongs to the classical tradition of twentieth-century painting. From within an old and stable art form, Johns experiments with completely diverse pictorial references and with all of the material left behind by analytic abstraction, picking up where Abstract Expressionism left off. His paintings are reactionary rather than conservative in as much as they seem concerned with a genuine revival and claim to get around formalist and ideological dead ends by renewing ancient forms. Yet the work continually challenges its own existence and casts an amused but serious eye on its own time. The work of Jasper Johns is undoubtedly autonomous and self-referential and yet, because of its many diverse elements, it manages to maintain a critical edge on the outside world and never stops questioning its own validity.

---

1. *Les États-Unis de la peinture*, Paris: Éd. du Seuil, 1986.
2. *Pop' Art*, London: Thames and Hudson, 1966.

A turning point in history

If we skim over American art history, we discover an art which from 1900 on is deeply influenced by both English painting and Impressionism, but also an art in search of its own authenticity, an authenticity that only a few rare artists will find.

Prendergast owes much to the Symbolists and the Pre-Raphaelites, John Sloan, Everett Shinn and Robert Henri are merely gifted disciples. Fauvism, Cubism and Futurism are reflected in the work of those artists who came to Europe to study, such as Max Weber. One of the personalities in the foreground, who will not be recognized until much later, was Georgia O'Keeffe who, from 1919 on, practised a poetic and powerful abstraction. While John Marin and Arthur Dove are marvelous painters, encouraged by the European avant-garde, they did not open any new doors or engender any new movements. At the same time a realist tradition flourished — with Edward Hopper as its most famous representative — and continued to do so in many different forms, from Expressionist and Surrealist inspired poetry to the strict photo realism of Ben Sloan, Andrew Wyeth and Stuart Davis.

The first American painter to call himself such was undoubtedly Arshile Gorky, from a Turkish-Armenian background, who came on the scene as early as 1936 during the WPA (Federal Art Project), and quickly established his importance with an abstract and suggestive style, a sense of architectural composition and mural painting. At that time, De Kooning had yet to prove himself.

Lee Krasner was known as early as 1939, before Jackson Pollock. Everyone at the time was strongly influenced by Picasso, but Mondrian, Léger, Herbin, and Hélion were also respected and served as models for the abstract, geometric, post-Cubist art that has had so many imitators.

The emergence of a group of Abstracts Expressionist painters just after the Second World War, who were not tied to any of the major European aesthetic movements, put an end to provincial American art once and for all.

Two major causes can be attributed to this upheaval: the Depression, which brought artists together to collaborate on important projects financed by the WPA, often ultimately leading to a better understanding of themselves; and the war, which forced many of Europe's greatest painters to seek refuge in the United States, where they quickly established ties with New York's Intelligentsias and were warmly welcomed.

Imagine the arrival of Josef Albers, Lyonel Feininger, Lazlo Moholy-Nagy, Naum Gabo; the architects Walter Gropius, Marcel Breuer and Mies van der Rohe; not to mention Mondrian and Amédée Ozenfant, the theoretician of Purism, into this environment still under the influence of Surrealism, though granted it was not always well assimilated. And then in a second wave came: Matta, Dalí, Masson and Ernst. Even if recognition was late in coming, the effect, from 1950 on, was overwhelming. Pollock, Kline, Gorky, Motherwell and De Kooning quickly absorbed the European contributions and then proceeded to go beyond them. Max Ernst's marriage to the heiress Peggy Guggenheim, an enterprising art dealer known for bringing exiled Europeans and isolated Americans together, can be seen as a point of convergence between the two sides of the Atlantic.

An American school was born: Abstract Expressionism. First recognized by American collectors and museums, it was soon famous throughout the world, due to large exhibitions and essays by several eminent critics, notably

Clement Greenberg, Harold Rosenberg and William Rubin.

It is in this context that Jasper Johns and others began to paint. From the very start they rejected their precursors and searched for something more current, something that would present a more accurate image of their country and civilization.

Traditional French scholarship, handed down from Taine, postulates that one begin a study with the subject's origins —his heredity and education — in order to grasp the obscure paths of creativity that make a man like any other realize his full potential and rise to the heights of glory. Unfortunately, we know very little about Jasper Johns' formative years and practically nothing about his ancestors. When we put together the information provided by his various biographies and the rare facts that he himself has offered about the first part of his life, we can safely deduce that his childhood was disrupted by many moves. While most of the important books on Johns have bibliographies, few include biographical information.

All of this points to an artist who is exceptionally reticent and who does not want to indulge in revealing his private life. But mystery encourages inquisitiveness. We will resist the temptation and respect his privacy.

It seems that we are going to have to be content with the few concessions he has offered. John Cage has been his main, if not only, confidant, and it is amusing to note that the quotations found sprinkled throughout books and articles on Johns are for the most part extracted from an essay by the great composer, published in 1964 in the catalogue for his exhibition at the Jewis Museum. Given that the source — a friend, a confidant and a supporter — is entirely reliable, we have not hesitated to make use of these excerpts ourselves. Jasper Johns has also recorded notes on paper: memory aides for his work as well as little poems that reveal the cryptic detours of his thoughts and may help clarify certain aspects of his work. But these texts, when read out of context, remain somewhat abstruse.

For information about the first twenty years of his life, we have relied on the official biographies, in particular the one by Anna Brooke.[3]

Jasper Johns is a man from the South. But to a lady who asked him if he was a "southern gentleman," he answered: "No, I'm trash." His response certainly expresses the uprooted, wandering and solitary nature of his childhood. Born in 1930 in Augusta, Georgia, he was brought up in Allendale, South Carolina by relatives — his grandparents, an aunt and an uncle — after his parents divorced. Up until the fourth grade, he went to school in Columbia, and then lived in various other communites with his mother, step-father, two half-sisters and a half-brother.

In 1949 he left for New York and took classes at a commercial art school, most likely in advertising. He turned down a scholarship that was offered to him, out of pity no doubt, because his work was not appreciated. He worked as a messenger and as a clerk. A call from the army gave him the opportunity to discover Japan, where he will later return with John Cage. Back in New York, he was entitled to a college scholarship, but quit Hunter College after twenty-four hours and went to work in a bookstore.

Towards the end of 1954, his friend Suzi Gablik introduced him to Robert Rauschenberg, five years his elder, and also to John Cage. That same year he left his Upper Manhattan address on 83rd Street to move downtown, and along with Robert Rauschenberg, made a living by designing window displays for department stores, including Tiffany's. His studio on Pearl Street was next door to Rachel Rosenthal's and not far from Robert

---

3. See *Chronology* in Richard Francis, *Johns*, New York: Abbeville Press, 1984.

c

d

a. Marcel Duchamp.

b. Eugène Delacroix:
Liberty Guiding the People. 1830.
Oil on canvas, 102¼ × 128 in.
(260 × 325 cm).

c. Josef Albers:
Homage to the square.

d. John Cage. c. 1960.

Rauchenberg's on Fulton Street. Sometime later, Rauschenberg moved into Rachel Rosenthal's loft. This was the beginning of a long historical relationship.

Legend has it that in 1955, Johns, who was already painting, destroyed all of his work. It seems that both Rauschenberg and Johns were taken with, if not exactly iconoclastic fervor, a powerful impulse to make a clean sweep of the past, even if it was only a symbolic one. Rauschenberg erased a drawing by De Kooning. Why? Perhaps the older artist's distinct style bothered him or got in the way of his own development. Or perhaps he wanted to break with the past, with instinctual and expressive art. These explanations are superficial at best, yet the gesture does seem symptomatic of their generation. In any case, these kinds of acts, recorded by witnesses, remain a perplexing characteristic of the age.

Only four works survived Johns' act of destruction. This "liquidation" corresponds to the start of a new period, to a radical change, to a rebirth. It is at this moment that Jasper Johns painted his first flag (*White Flag*; Fig. 5), his first targets, (*Target with Four Faces* ; Fig. 2), his first series of numbers, *1, 2, 5* and *7*, and made his first plaster casts. This is a period of intense activity for Johns, a veritable explosion, as though he had been aroused by some kind of revelation. In fact, this is not far from the explanation he himself provides later on when he tells us that he saw himself painting a flag in a dream.

Robert Rauschenberg

Concerning this "revelation," any number of interpretations are possible. One can imagine the young provincial artist, recently arrived from the South, just barely making ends meet by doing window displays, meeting John Cage for the first time. His elder by almost twenty years, a student of Schönberg, a thinker, a philosopher and a venturer before being a composer, he must have opened undreamt-of horizons for the young painter. Anything is possible. Johns had to discover the world on his own and as he found out, the greatest riches are often hidden inside of the most humble objects, the ones that we no longer see because we have looked at them so many times.

Johns has claimed that he does not like to draw, and that he uses flags and targets because they are already drawn and all he has to do is copy them. This sounds like a provocation. But then it was said during a period, between 1954 and 1955, that witnessed the historic birth of Pop Art.

What is Pop Art? It is most certainly not popular art, but rather an art that uses objects from everyday life for its main material. These objects function as both a medium and a tool, as they will for Arman, César and the French Neo-Realists. Even in the case of Marcel Duchamp, the bicycle wheel and the urinal are not ends in themselves, but a means by which to convey a message. If these objects were not assembled, arranged, organized, modified, and sometimes painted or molded by the artist, who thereby gives breaths new life into them, they would not be what they are today; Duchamp's bicycle wheel, like Claes Oldenburg's *Blue Pants*, would be in the garbage dump, worn out, useless and devoid of any meaning, instead of in the world's greatest museums. Pop Art, like all aesthetic movements from the past few centuries, was only named, defined and theorized after a gap of several years. In 1955 Johns and Rauschenberg heralded its arrival, but remained within the tradition of painting.

If Pop Art is almost always considered a specifically American movement, it is wrongly so. The idea of exploiting the image of consumer society, without denouncing or attacking it, as will happen during the Sixties, appeared simultaneously on both sides of the Atlantic. While on the eve of the Sixties, French artists were creating a "new figuration" loaded with political ulterior motives, English artists were borrowing "popular" images from advertising in order to give their work the power of suggestion, strong connotations that should have made it accessible to the public at large. But art remained a coded language only understood by the initiated.

While Robert Rauschenberg was working on his first *Combine Paintings*, Paolozzi, Richard Hamilton, Allen Jones and Peter Blake, were gluing images from advertisements on to their canvases in Great Britain. Kitaj, Phillips and Hockney, with varied objectives and different styles, also participated in the appropriation of popular culture, specifically that of advertising. Yet America was unaware of what was going on in Europe. According to Lucy Lippard, Pop Art was not a movement with popular roots, but rather, a reaction against the rarefied character of Abstract Expressionism and a manifestation of a new desire to have a positive attitude towards contemporary society. It was a youthful outlook that appropriated images for personal ends. The fact is that most of New York's artist from that period were relatively isolated and Warhol's silk screens were in no way influenced by Lichtenstein's cartoons.

While Johns is an extremely perceptive painter and was perfectly aware of what was going on around him, the adventure he embarked on was ultimately a solitary one. Does this perception of the outside world explain the insertion of found objects into his paintings? Had he seen Rauschenberg's *White Painting with Numbers* from 1949? The numbers climb up the painting on various ladder-like configurations scattered in all different directions, in a graphic disorder that is justified by the aesthetic impact. There is even a star in the lower right-hand corner!

We cannot say with any conviction that Rauschenberg had a direct influence on Johns, but we do know that their meeting has had many repercussions and that the older artist played the role of catalyst in John's revelation about the possibilities of painting. Rauschenberg will go further than Johns in his use of varied, if not peculiar, materials that he transforms and endows with a hereditary nobility. From the very start, Johns, resolutely personal, has been more concerned with painting in and of itself, a tradition he has enriched with his own original style. Jasper John's is, without a doubt, the most painterly of all the Pop Painters — he is first and foremost a painter. We can even go so far as to say that the subject itself does not count in his work, that it is merely a pretext for stylistic exercises. After all, what could be more banal than a target, a flag, a map, or a series of stenciled numbers or letters?

Two different hypotheses can be presented as to why Jasper Johns chose such neutral themes: Perhaps he wanted to separate himself from the tradition of abstract painting, which is entirely plausible, at least in the beginning when he was associated with the Pop movement by both critics and dealers. On the other hand, these subjects might contain some kind of message and not be as neutral as they appear. Johns does not choose just any map or any flag, but a map of the United States and the American flag. Given that Pop Art appeared as, if not the first, at least one of the first, specifically American movements, his choice of these emblems takes on an entirely different meaning.

Let's for a moment do the impossible and put ourselves in the artist's place. What can you do with a flag? In 1954, ten years after the war, the choices were somewhat limited, especially if you are an American, and moreover, from the South. Johns served in the U.S. Army in Japan at the beginning of the Fifties. He is neither an anarchist, nor a revolutionary. He is a painter. He was undoubtedly irritated by the connections that were made between his work and that of his contemporaries who would, and not without reason, be called "Pop." The denunciation of an omnipresent society that imposed its national and humanitarian values was already in the air. But we have not yet reached the attack on consumer society that will flourish in the late Sixties.

An original technique

In order to be a part of his time, to fit in with his generation, Johns had to use the most banal, the most common, the most ordinary subjects. There was nothing to fight against, few causes to support. So he turned to the public realm, to those objects that confront us on a daily basis and whose meanings he could distort. The flag seemed as good a choice as any, and since he is American, why not the flag of his country?

From within the country many interpreted his choice as a symbol of nationalism, and from the outside, as a symbol of imperialism. Both views underestimate Johns and his intentions. He is first and foremost a painter, and any subject will do as long as it is simple and does not take away from his sole preoccupation, which is to paint: to put colors side by side on the canvas, to cover its surface and make it come alive. The star-spangled banner provided the perfect pretext.

It is important to note that the flag is always, without exception, painted flat, as though it were laid out on a table or tacked to the wall. Of all of the many representations of the flag that appear in painting, this case is unique. The flags depicted in paintings throughout history, from the banners found in medieval miniatures, to the *Quatorze Juillet* paintings by Marquet or Dufy, are always portrayed in action, as rallying symbols waving in the breeze, held up high, leading soldiers to the battlefield. Carried on top of a pole, whipped by the wind, the flag in these paintings is never a rectangle, but a flowing cloth, capable of taking on any number of forms. No two look alike, except for the flags painted by Jasper Johns. Paradoxically, a flag by Johns is at once an image of the flag, and the flag itself, painted on cloth, as all flags are. As he himself has said, he does not have to look for, invent, or draw his motifs. They are already there, never changing, even if the number of stars has gone from forty-eight to fifty since he painted his first flags. The fact that he sometimes used different colored backgrounds for his flags (one of the first being orange) only reinforces the

Marcel Duchamp: *Genre Allegory (George Washington)*. 1943.
Assemblage, 21 × 16 in. (53,2 × 40,5 cm).

theory that with Johns' it is above all a matter of painting. At first he respected the original colors (most of the time) but later began to stray from them, giving free rein to his fantasies. One of the results was a white flag, not uniformly white, but painted within a monochromatic scale that creates an exceptional visual impact. The flag is essential to him in that not only is it the source of his fame, but more importantly, it provides a framework on which he can freely express his chromatic visions. He will use the flag motif throughout his career, including his most recent work, where it appears as a quotation. Does the fact that the flag is such a "noble" pretext place him within the larger pictorial tradition? Up until the explosion of abstract art, painting that is purely self-referential, all of the great artists indulged their obsession for painting, and in a thousand different ways. Seen in this light, the flag functions for Johns much as the monsters did for Goya during his black period; religious themes for El Greco and countless others; and landscapes for Poussin as well as for the Impressionists. In each case the subject matter is subservient, colors play freely and the content is enriched. Each of these artists, including Johns, have their own unique style. According to the French critic Catherine Francblin, the flag can be compared to *The Virgin and the Child* motif. To a large degree, Johns' talent, and the reason for his success, lies in the technique that he developed.

The material he uses is the result of a long preparation in which he mixes collage and encaustic, a substance that was abandoned in the Middle Ages. Since the mid-nineteenth century, encaustic is usually associated with the maintenance of parquet floors, at least in France. Artists have used this procedure in the past, which consists of mixing colored pigments with melted wax before applying it to a canvas or wood panel. This must be done while the mixture is still hot, in order to give the wax the necessary fluidity. Johns, however, proceeds in two stages. He does not work directly on the linen canvas, but covers it first with newspaper. This creates a smooth surface, streaked with columns of newsprint, unreadable under the paint but still visible in certain spots, creating a reverberation typical of his work. There is a certain preciosity in this long and patient process, but also an extraordinary richness. By comparison the objects he uses — the predella made from wooden crates, the plaster casts, the cans and hangers — are simple to make. A good pair of pliers, an awl and some wire will do the trick.

We have yet to analyze his choice of objects for the plaster casts. Most often they are fragments of the human body: heads, mouths, legs. His painted bronzes are done with a classical technique that he will use at different times throughout his career. If strict chronology is the best way to analyze an artist's development, it is invalid when it comes to Jasper Johns. Presumably he found all of his major themes, as though by revelation, between 1954 and 1955, and since that time has merely created variations, a little like Mozart, whom an impertinant critic has accused of having composed the same symphony thirty-seven times. What a stupid misinterpretation! What disregard for an artist's work and what blindness towards painting (and music)! Only a complete lack of insight could make anyone believe that he actually knows the work of Jasper Johns after having seen several examples of the flags, targets, numbers and letters on display in a museum.

In 1972 John's work underwent a change, when in a sort of homage to his elders, including Jackson Pollock, he began his *crosshatching* series. This occured after his maps and many other great works such as *Studio* (Fig. 52), *Harlem Light* (Fig. 57), *Voice I, Voice II* (Fig. 62), and *According to What* (Fig. 48), not to mention the many *Untitleds* (Fig. 49). In order to fully appreciate the infinite variations and nuances that make each flag painting a unique work, a large number of them should be gathered together and exhibited in a museum. As John Cage has said, an American flag painted by Johns is as beautiful as a "sonnet." He elaborated: "Beginning, that is, with structure, the division of the all in two parts corresponding to the parts of the flag, the painting was made with both obscure and clarified the underlying structure. Precedent is in poetry, the sonnet: by means of language, caesurae, iambic pentameter, licence and rimes, to obscure and clarifying the grant division of the fourteen lines into eight and six." The composer, who has eyes as well as ears, speaks as a poet. He understands rythm, caesura and modulation. The red, white and blue that Johns used are

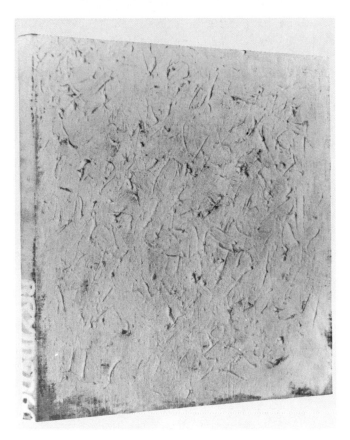

Robert Ryman: *Untitled*. 1960.

The early paintings (from 1954 and the years immediately following), show that Jasper Johns, who at that time rejected any visible traces of personal motifs disguised in paint, is a visionary colorist. *Green Target* (Fig. 4), and *Tango* (Fig. 7), both from 1955, with their minute variations of green and blue, can be understood as chromatic investigations. As always, the paint is not applied directly to the canvas, but to a layer of paper which has been carefully pasted on, in different thicknesses. The green in *Green Target* is luminous because it covers an acid yellow that still shows through in spots, as does a grey-black, which turns out to be the newspaper. The green of *Green Target* is also luminous because the paint, applied to the canvas with a knife no doubt, does not have a smooth surface but is rather a succession of unequal layers diversely arranged. The effect is similar to that of a cut diamond that reflects the light from various angles and lends force to the colors. The same can be said about the blue in *Tango*, but in this case something else has been added. This is the first of many paintings to have an inscription. It is a single word: "Tango," which refers to the particular shade of blue used and gives the painting its name. The inscriptions is discreet, boxed into the upper left-hand corner, painted in the same kind of paint and in the same blue color, but slightly darker, with the result that at first glance one does not notice it at all. Only when the eye stops to linger and travels over the entire surface in order to fully appreciate the various modulations, does the inscription become clearly visible.

Philosophic and artistic theories seem insignificant when confronted by such works. The artist's intentions are clear: creation without ulterior motives, only the painting itself counts.

Yet Jasper Johns was not satisfied with being the bridge between Abstract Expressionism and the Pop Art which was beginning to surface. He seemed anxious to give a *meaning* to his work, to those canvases that look like large "pieces" of paintings to us, which is exactly what the critics said about those great works exhibited in the Paris Salons at the end of the nineteenth century.

His titles are often taken from the inscriptions or objects inserted in the paintings. For example, the painting *Drawer* (Fig. 9), includes the front piece of a drawer, *Book* (Fig. 11), quite naturally, is a painted book, and *Canvas* (Fig. 8), is a beautifully painted surface of a canvas that has a stretcher glued to the center.

The *Flag* and *Target* paintings develop over the years. As one of his critics has pointed out, Jasper Johns does not paint series, but periodically resumes his favorite themes and with each new canvas creates a new painting that has nothing to do with the preceeding one, the only true similarity being the motif which serves as his pretext.

What kind of commentary can one make (without becoming boring and pedantic) about these canvases that all have one thing in common yet are never the same? There are many divergences in the painter's line of development, such as *Alley Oop*, an orange abstract painting he did in 1958 that is in Robert Rauschenberg's collection.

never the standard official colors. He creates a new painting each time, either by variations in color or by modifying the shape, as is the case with *Flag Above White with Collage,* in which the strict rectangle of its model is arranged in a different format. His material and brush strokes are clean and geometric when he wants them to be and can evoke Mondrian's technique, who never did paint "smoothly," as those who have only seen his reproductions might believe. When Johns gave in to his impulses, to his lyrical outbursts, he anticipated Robert Ryman, and the spectator discovers in his pure monochromes, an ocean of waves emitted from some disturbing depth. In his obsession for painting and for proving the infinite possibilites of a single theme, he even went so far as to superimpose three flags on top of one another in such a way that their stretchers cast shadows and create relief.

Johns' insistence on multiplying the variations and experiences of a single theme brings to mind another artist, Josef Albers. Fleeing from the Weimar Bauhaus, he came to New York where he carried on with his work, taught courses, tried to pass on his experiences and exposed his paintings. In 1950 when I asked Albers, who painted squares for more than twenty years, the entire last part of his career, when he thought he would take on a new theme, he answered: "Oh, I'm far from having exhausted the possibilities of the square."

Johns also discovered the graphic impact of the coat hanger, the simple wire kind that comes back from the dry cleaners. Without it, many of his paintings and drawings would be abstract works. The sudden intrusion of the coat hanger, reduced to its most minimal reality, whether in negative on a thick surface, covered by brush strokes, or, as is the case in several paintings, the object itself, gives the work an entirely new meaning. Here is the presence of an ordinary, banal, functional, everyday — dare we say it — "popular" object, which can only be understood as a manifestation of Pop aesthetics.

In 1958 a new development occurs. He starts making three dimensional work. The juxtaposition of painting and sculpture had already been made when he inserted plaster casts into his canvases. But this time something else happens. In what will amount to a meaningful and decisive act, he takes an everyday object and transforms it into a museum piece. It is not a question of modelling or of sculpting, methods he would most certainly loathe, but let's not jump ahead. As Johns would say, one must not confuse "looking" with "shooting." While this admonishment seems especially apt for his *Target* paintings, it should also be kept in mind for the rest of his work. His views on criticism are well known. For Johns, the critic "aims" while the true art lover "looks." In this light his *Target* paintings can be seen not only as an objectification of the critic's point of view but also as a type of spring board that sends the critic's look to him. But these *Targets* are paintings and therefore objects to be looked at. As Johns himself has said: "What's been done is something to look at." In other words, Johns is concerned with creating an object to be looked at, not an object that will reflect outside experiences, nor an object that will demarcate a particular point in art history. Johns' presence behind this object is completely incidental. This is undoubtedly where his obsession to fill up the canvas's entire surface, to sweep it with paint, comes from. These remarks are also applicable to the paintings with numbers and letters.

In 1955, Johns made his first number paintings. Did he begin with *Zero* as in the lithographs? Given the number's symmetry he would not have to draw it backwards. *Figure 5*, painted in 1955, is a vigorous painting, done in a more elaborate style than those that will come later. The large brush strokes impose themselves with force, underlining the fact that this is painting, not mathematics. One cannot say with any certainty just where the number came from. Outside of a reference to the date in which it was painted, the most plausible explanation can be found in a poem by William Carlos Williams called *The Great Figure*:

Among the rain	*tense*
and lights	*unheeded*
I saw the figure 5	*to gong clangs*
in gold	*siren howls*
on a red	*and wheels rumbling*
firetruck	*through the dark city.*
moving	*(1921)*

According to the French translator of Williams Carlos Williams, this poem was the inspiration for Charles Demuth's *I Saw the Figure 5 in Gold*. And it must have been this painting that then inspired Robert Indiana to paint *American Dream* (1963) and Jasper Johns to paint *Figure 5* (1955).

Whatever the case may be, the question of origins is always a problematic one and will not take us very far. As with the targets and the flags, the number "5" is merely a pretext for his main obsession, painting itself. As in the poem, the "5" in the painting appears as a flash, a poetic image that rises up from a chaotic background. It is also a figure of rationality.

One can only be amazed by the richness and diversity that Johns has created from such a neutral theme. From the large, isolated numbers, to the tables where endless rows of numbers line up, the paintings are never monotonous, but on the contrary, are continuously renewed. The painting itself is what counts. What difference does it make where his inspiration came from? The artist, through a process that must be time consuming, paints an extremely thick surface, causing the vewer to forget the numbers in order to focus on the shimmering modulations of color. American critics have tried to analyze the type of numbering he has chosen. Apparently the question never even occured to Johns. He painted the standardized numbers that he saw most often, very likely those from price tags. In the end, the question is not extremely relevant since the subject of his work is not the numbers but the painting.

Jasper Johns' number paintings become surfaces for meditation, much like Mark Tobey's paintings, with whom he must feel some affinity. Writers can ramble on forever about the symbolism of his numbers. But as my colleague Catherine Francblin has sensibly noted, numbers do not exist in nature and are not things that can be apprehended by the senses. Rather, they are the result of an abstract operation and have no existence outside of their function. As soon as they are painted, they become useless, stripped of their function, and it is only then that we truly *see* them, rediscovering one of our sense that is often obstructed by our intellectual capacities.

The number paintings first appeared in 1955 and the alphabets the following year. 1956 was also the year he developed his *Surrounding Color Fields*, those luminous and colored fields, such as his *Flag on Orange Field* (Fig. 10).

Encaustic remained his medium of choice, as can be seen from *Grey Alphabet* painted in 1956.

All of these paintings were exhibited at the Jewish Museum, in his first important show. It was here that Leo Castelli, who would become his dealer, saw Johns' work for the first time. The outcome of their encounter was his first solo exhibition at the Leo Castelli Gallery in 1958 and to his inclusion in the Venice Biennale in 1964. Fame and international recognition came very quickly to Johns, even if it was his friend Robert Rauschenberg who won the prize at the Biennale, under circumstances that gave rise to a polemic.

Was this sudden glory the result of a misunderstanding? Did the public give too much importance to his technical gimmicks and the voluntary banality of his subjects? At that time, few people actually saw his paintings. Only the stance, the gesture, in short, the politics — not always cultural, mind you — were noticed, and the flag theme received much attention from those critics whose only approach to a work is a sociological one. As Pierre Restany has remarked: "The form was taken for the content."

Johns manages to unite in a single theme all of the different ways to attract the public. He paints with undeniable brilliance and uses a twentieth-century technique: encaustic. His themes are resolutely modern and no longer have anything to do with the history of painting. Yet, can we rightfully call these numbers a theme? Or, are they simply numerical signs used within the realm of painting, with no concrete reality and only an abstract reference? Numbers are present everywhere in contemporary society, on our calculators and computers. Everything, or almost everything, can be conveyed numerically. Johns does not stick to one number in his work, but exploits an entire system, rich with possible combinations, whose every element refers to an infinite number of things. And of course, the same can be said for the alphabet. Given the neutrality of Johns' motifs, anyone can come up with their own interpretation, define their own hermeneutics, but unfortunately, this will only serve to take them far away from the painting.

In Europe, misunderstandings of American art were common. Johns' exhibitions at the Gallery Rive-Droite, directed by Jean Lacarde, were interpreted in many different ways and the inclusion of his work at the International Exposition of Surrealism at Daniel Cordier towards the end of 1959, side by side with Rauschenberg and Stanckiewicz, and sponsored by Duchamp, only added to the confusion. This in particular explains that infamous epithet attached to Robert Rauschenberg's work, "neo-dada." American art amazed Europeans but they did not understand it.

This was not the case in the United States where *Time* magazine would declare: "Jasper Johns, 29, is a brand new darling of the art world, bright, brittle, avant-garde. A year ago he was practically unknown; since then he has had a sellout show in Manhattan, has exhibited in Paris and Milan, was the only American to win a painting prize at the Carnegie International and has seen three of his paintings bought for Manhattan's Museum of Modern Art."

That same year, Johns painted a series of numbers, *0-9* (Figs. 21, 22); *Shade* (Fig. 24), a strange and dark work, almost expressive; and *Device Circle*, a very colorful allegory in which he included, as he will often do later (Fig. 42), the title of the painting. The materials he used were familiar to him and the circular movements recall the *Targets*, but in this case the circle is so well incorporated into the composition that it almost disappears, a vain pretext for a play of color and gestural effects.

Around this time, Johns, already established in the New York art world, began to distance himself from it. 1960 was a year of intense activity and left him feeling the need to withdraw. To this end he did not exhibit for several years and left for Edisto Beach, South Carolina, his home state.

In *Zero Through Nine* (Fig. 32), *Out of the Window*; and *Painting with Two Balls* (Fig. 26), colors explode. This outburst is new for Johns. At the very same time that he is painting so many works in nuances of grey, he produces red, blue and yellow paintings. On one of them the names of the colors are written: orange, white, red, grey and blue. These names do not correspond to the color on which they are positioned, but are blended in with the painting. Johns seems to be toying with the idea of caption, of providing supplementary material for the viewer who does not know how to identify the colors, or who sees the painting in a black and white reproduction. Once again, he reaffirms the painting's autonomy, its refusal to be co-opted into a discursive category. Names of colors are linguistic signs and cannot be blended together to produce the name of a new color. If the words are positioned in contradiction to the chromatic reality, they nonetheless harmonize with the composition. The first paintings to use this idea are *False Start* (Fig. 23) and *Jubilee* (Fig. 25). How should this decidedly not "false start" be interpreted? Perhaps it is the representation of a spontaneous but perfectly controlled process, reduced to its most simple expression, in which colors are used in order to produce values and the gesture that brings these colors to the canvas is hidden by the explosion.

Red, Yellow and Blue will be used as leit-motifs throughout a long series of particularly dynamic and jubilant paintings.

According to several critics, primary colors represent origins. But what origins? The word is used here in its global sense, i.e., the origin of the world as well as that of painting. Johns is familiar with both the work and theories of Mondrian. Grey materializes the continuity of the spectrum when it is juxtaposed with infra-red and infra-violet. The effects of discontinuous addition or subtraction are well known. For example: yellow plus blue makes green, and the reverse is also true: green minus yellow makes blue.

As we have seen with the targets, the map of the United States serves as a framework on which he can develop brilliant and sparkling variations. The *Map* paintings are at once the image of American painting free of its European origins, and paintings of America. The names of the states are written out in standard type characters and are extremely evocative.

These inscriptions have several roles. They refer to an outside reality; they contribute to an abstract composition inasmuch as they are colored brush strokes; and, since they are words, they have a meaning, and insist on the fact that this is not an imaginary or gratuitous composition, but the map of one of the most powerful countries in the world.

Three dimensional work

In 1958 Johns began to work in three dimensions. He had already gone beyond painting when he inserted plaster casts into his canvases. But this time his process is different in that it consists of taking an ordinary object out of its usual setting and transforming it into a museum object. These pieces are not so much sculptures, or sculptures by a painter, as they are a series of both ironic and serious comments on painting. In some ways they are closer to cartoons that deal with the exchange value of objects and the art object as commodity, and expose the myth of the artist and of the critic.

In as much as these three dimensional works occupy a separate position within Johns' career, they warrant a separate chapter. In some ways they can be viewed as Johns' contribution to Pop Art, which is not to say that they should be placed under the label of Pop Art, for reasons we shall discuss.

Between his bronzified objects and his paintings with objects, there is not only a difference in medium, but also in intent. If a Johns painting is a discourse on painting, it is also a testimony of brilliance, and belongs in the annals of great art. The bronzes, on the other hand, make fun of the dignity of art and do not fall into any formal category.

The value of the object differs from one case to the other. The inserted object can either blend in with the painting or take on one of two possible roles. It can function as the subject, standing in for its own representation and providing a bridge between reality and the pictorial universe, or it can serve to vitalize the pictorial matter. The difference between these two different modes of collage is the same as the difference between Cubist collage and Surrealist collage. With Picasso and Braque, the paper — a piece of newspaper, a tobacco pack — is chosen for its artistic qualities and is considered to be equal to a painted image. Braque, moreover, painted fake collages in *trompe-l'oeil*. Thus, one forgets the nature of the material in order to consider the harmony of the composition, the nuances of its materials, etc.

In the surrealist collage *La Femme 100 têtes* by Max Ernst for example, the cut up and borrowed image exists for itself, for what it represents. Its meaning does not change and would remain the same even if it were taken out of its context and worked into a visual poem.

What is the relationship of Johns' three dimesional work to Pop Art, and to the object in general? Whether we consider it as an object chosen for its artistic qualities or for its function, the outcome is the same: any object chosen by the artist, touched by his hand, becomes a museum object. The uniform treatment to which Johns submits his objects still remains problematic. American Pop artists practiced what Oldenburg called a "double look" vis-à-vis the object, "both for and against". The reflection on the hyper-mediatization of art, on the pervasive diffusion of images, was accompanied by a joyous celebration of objects which were often representative of American society. Wesselman's or Dine's use of objects is at once

a mockery of painting and a glorification of the object. This is not at all the case with Johns's bronzes. They appear as somewhat ironic echoes, a similar but darker vision than that of Pop Art. *Savarin* (Fig. 78) makes fun of the myth of the artist, whose importance greatly escalated out of proportion during the era of Action Painting. The same can be said for the painting *The Fool's House*, in which the broom that looks as though it had painted a blue streak on the canvas is an ironic substitute for the brush. Its shakey movement seems to determine the composition without any help from the artist.

With the Ballantine ale cans, cast in bronze and then painted, Johns points to the absurdity of the painter's work and questions the very idea of representation, as many of his contemporaries were also doing. Behind their hoax-like appearance, these works anticipate certain post-conceptual methods. Legend has it that the idea for the Ballantine cans came to Johns after he had heard the off-hand remark of a critic who claimed that Castelli could sell anything, including a can of beer. Siding with the critic, he carried out the pointless task of painting bronze in order to duplicate ordinary ale cans, endowing them with the added value of artistic work in order to turn them into art. The copy becomes more expensive than the original because the artist's intervention increases its commercial value.

With Johns, familiar objects become archeological finds, evidence of a long lost society and therefore worthy of a museum. But what kind of museum? A museum of modern art seems less appropriate than a museum of archeology. Johns has written the history of the past for the future. The light bulb is to the twentieth century what the flint was to the Stone Age. Without this modest piece of stone, how would we live? We would be condemned to extinction or regress a millenium in the history of humanity.

Johns engaged in a full production for each of his objects. He projects us into an uncertain future. Is the object we see in the museum the thing itself or a bronze cast of it?

In the end it does not really matter. Only the thoughts and feelings provoked by actually viewing the works are important. These reactions are determined by the way in which Johns has dealt with the modest glass bulb embedded in a copper base.

One of them[4] is resting on a bed of pliable matter that could be dirt or clay. The other[5] is bare and isolated, existing on its own. Its surface is not the smooth translucent one of glass but that of cast metal, with all its bumps and irregularities, and a twisted electrical wire juts out, as though someone had severed it with a pair of pliers.

It seems to be telling a story, if only to itself, about an attempt to modernize. A specialist has voluntarily

---

4. *Light Bulb*, 1958.

5. *Light Bulb II*, 1958.

destroyed all earlier sources of light in order to install higher peformance models.

A drawing from that same year reaffirms Johns' desire to put the object on stage: highlighted with subtle lighting in a neutral decor, the lines of graphite appear as curtains to the privileged site.

The first *Flashlight* is a large one mounted on its base like a rocket or a missile. It attests to the kind of civilization we live in, if only as a mocking symbol. Johns manages to transform this ordinary household item into an offensive weapon, endowing it with immeasurable force.

Flashlight II lies on a bent papier mâché base and is stained with tarnish and rust, as though it had spent twenty years at the bottom of the ocean. Used and abandoned, it can no longer serve any purpose other than to testify to what it once was. It is ready for the museum.

Two years later, in 1960, Johns produced something of a remake, but with different intentions. This time he painted a bronze cast of a new ligth bulb, resting on a phosphorescent blue base. It is no longer a facsimile of an excavated object, but a ready (re)made, *à la* Duchamp. What is the meaning of this object that no longer lights up unless by reflecting outside light? A light bulb that does not produce its own light no longer makes sense. Its only meaning comes from the context in which it is placed. The whole question of light in painting and sculpture is wrapped up in this brilliant metaphor of the situation of the art object. And the different versions of the light bulb only reinforce this notion.

Does Johns carry out all these variations on a theme, the ale cans and the light bulbs, for himself alone, or does he do it in order to provoke his public and those critics who analyse every minute variation in his work?

One piece in particular bluntly states his point of view on criticism: *The Critic Sees* (1961), made out of plaster, metal and glass. A pair of glasses peer out from the plaster, but instead of lenses there are two open mouths, their teeth exposed. These mouths seem to be saying something, but what? They are speaking the language of art criticism, a language that obstructs vision, not unlike, perhaps, the one am I developing here. These mouths also look as though they are ready to eat, to devour the artist. In short, the critic is a mouth before being a pair of eyes or a mind.

Not only does painting engage sight and intellect, it also provokes sensations that are often difficult to articulate. Action Painting added a new dimension, that of physical effort. By looking at the painting, the viewer decodes and feels the power of the painter's gesture.

I can easily imagine a variation of this piece, in which there would be a mouth behind one lens and an ear behind the other.

Jasper Johns, however, came up with a more original sequel: *The Critic Smiles* (Fig. 60), a simple toothbrush cast in bronze. Just where do his titles come from (outside of the many *Untitled* works)? From his sense of humor, his desire to provoke, a sudden idea, or are they the aftermath of late night conversations with friends?

One is continually reminded of his ties to Duchamp and John Cage, especially when it comes to this kind of "biting" cynicism.

Paul Valéry had already written: "Art lives only through words." During Johns' career the mediatization of art was emphasized. The critic does not look, he speaks.

Max Kozloff presents his own interpretation of this minor, but nonetheless striking work in his book on Johns.[6] Starting from the premise that things have no intrinsic value, Johns puts the mechanism of reflection into play. The work would be unimportant in and of itself if it did not cause the viewer to reflect, offering a wide range of possibilites as to how it can be looked at and contemplated, even if it contains no actual message. In this way it brings about a self discovery, an experience specific to the painter's work.

This phenomenon stems from the visual complexity of Johns' work. His objects are genuinely provocative. It is as though he is trying to test the imaginative capacities of the "voyeur."

One of his sculptures is a visual joke *à la* Duchamp. *High School Days* from 1964, is a plastic shoe covered in metal with a small round mirror on the toe. The mirror, like that of a sorcerer, seems capable of reflecting both the happy and unhappy memories of the highschool student. In this case it happens to be the trick of the sorcerer's apprentice who, by slipping the tip of his shoe under the girls' skirts, discovers their secrets. A highschool boy's practical joke: which explains the title. These works by Johns are always ambiguous and call for a certain amount of reading between the lines. The objects remain enigmatic, like the pastiche of a good student who, not wanting to be outdone by his master, gives himself the license to experiment.

To point out the fact that Johns has a predilection for using casts of the human body lends nothing to the understanding of his work. As we have already mentioned, Johns borrows or finds his objects. The cast is a convenient way to settle the question of the body in painting — of the heroism or crisis of the subject — from a formal as well as an existential point of view. His art is completely autonomous, without an outside purpose. His casts have a powerful impact. They come across as trophies, but as if they have been stripped bare.

Beyond the somewhat physical process involved in producing these art objects, can we claim that the work of art arouses the senses?

When it comes to *Light Bulb, Flash Light*, and the sculpmetal pieces, one has to wonder whether or not Johns was influenced by Marcel Duchamp. Just as the French artist had done several decades earlier, Johns takes an ordinary object, removes it from its social, economic and functional context, and turns it into a work of art. Johns made these works in 1958. However, he did not discover Robert Lebel's book on Duchamp until 1959, the year he would actually meet Duchamp through Nicolas Calas. But

6. *Jasper Johns*, New York: Abrams, 1967.

he won the grand prize of the 1958 Carnegie International in Pittsburg for painting and sculpture and had read Robert Motherwells book on Dada painters and poets. He first saw Duchamp's work at the Philadelphia Museum. Here the historian is confronted with a dilemma, not unlike the one that confronts the Picasso specialist concerning the *Demoiselles d'Avignon*. Did Picasso know about African art when he altered the figures on the right-hand side of the painting? The eminent experts have thrown up their hands in bewilderment and have admitted the possibility of a sixth sense a transcendental one.

Everything seemed to lead Johns to Duchamp. Not only do they share a similar curiosity, but approach and carry out their work in much the same way. Furthermore, John Cage, who knew Duchamp, had very likely let some of the French artist's ideas filter through his conversations with Johns.

The large works

Over the years Johns' strokes of genius and innovation multiplied. In 1961 he inserted objects into the painting called *Good Time Charley*. A yardstick moves across the canvas like a windshield wiper, and in its path, the painting becomes lighter, even if the work's predominant colors, in this case blue and grey, do not change. These kinds of semicircles are frequently reiterated in Johns' work. A quarter of a century later, in *Four Seasons*, we find the same principle applied with the same effectiveness.

This also holds true for *Device* (Fig. 42), painted the following year. Here two semicircles appear at the top of the composition, looking as though a windshield wiper had tried to wipe off the paint, but only suceeded in spreading it around.

Shortly after, he produced the *Skin* studies, which are anatomical fragments printed on paper with charcoal. As in lithography, he creates the printed composition by hand, a process that is similar to prehistoric painting. He uses an artistic technique close to the one archeologists employ for recording high reliefs. The paper is applied to the model's body and then evenly rubbed with graphite — in this case charcoal — causing the reliefs to appear in dark grey on a greyish surface, the body first having been coated with oil and sprinkled with graphite powder.

One of the most important skin studies is not a drawing but a lithograph, produced at ULAE in Los Angeles, called *Skin with O'Hara Poem*. The imprint of a body is surrounded by two open hands and the poems is reproduced on the right-hand side. Frank O'Hara, a close friend of Johns and to whom the work is dedicated, was not only a poet but also a curator at the Museum of Modern Art. Johns also cast the poet's foot in order to make a relief from it and dedicated another large piece to him: *O'Hara: In Memory of my Feelings* (1961). A diptych in shades of grey-blue, it has a dark mass on the upper left-hand side that ends in a table setting (a fork and a spoon linked by a wire). On the lower left-hand side the title of the works is painted in standard type letters. In 1973 he commited the offense of doing another skin study, but this time imprint is of his genitals.

The various *Divers* are among the most important works from 1963. They signal an innovation in that Johns introduced a figurative subject. A large "V" drawn in charcoal and pastel ends at the diver's hands — or are they his feet? Is the diver jumping in feet first, or diving in head first? Johns will use this subject in several paintings. For example, it appears in *Red, Yellow and Blue*, a large painting more than twelve feet across, divided into vertical sections where many of his favorite motifs appear: a semicircle in color, the color spectrum of grey, a pictogram of the diver who looks as though he is being thrown from a bridge, and an action painting violently colored in red, yellow and blue.

All of Johns' work, in its vast diversity, is self-referential. It continually turns back on itself and calls attention to its own existence. While it is self-consuming and plays with its own devices, it also steps back from them, in a movement towards self-exhaustion and schizophrenia. Perhaps it was just such a fear that pushed Johns to get away from his studio and spend several months in Hawaii.

This long vacation, spent with his friends John Cage and Lois Long, renewed his inspiration. While the works that he made upon returning cannot be said to constitute an actual turning point or rupture, they do reflect a "breath of fresh air." A work from that time, called *Souvenir*, is made up of diverse elements brought together on the canvas: a rear-view mirror, a flashlight, a canvas stretcher and a plate with his picture on it, surrounded by the words "Red," "Yellow" and "Blue," and this time the names of the colors and the colors themselves correspond. The story behind this work claims that the inspiration for it came to Johns during a John Cage concert in honor of the composer David Tudor. A woman in the audience who was holding a mirror happened to reflect one of the spotlights. At that moment Johns asked himself: "What will my next painting be?" Of course this does not explain the profound implications of the work. Once again, under the pretext of a souvenir portrait, Johns brilliantly plays with the elements of painting: the pictorial matter, the light, the subject or story, and both the symbolic and functional value of the mirror, which is not prospective, but retrospective. The various elements, some of which have already been used and thrown out, come back to the canvas in the form of ironic trophies. The plate is a revival of popular arts and crafts, its tinted colors seem to have nothing to do with the photo-booth quality of the image. This plate also evokes the various beheadings that haunt the history of painting, as though Johns were offering the viewer his head on a platter. As Johns has written in one of his notebooks, to look is both "to eat" and "be eaten". (A comment that is equally revealing in relation to *The Critic Sees*. The work can also be understood as a response to the public's fascination for the artist's body and demand for biographical information. But it is at the same time a reminder that these personal elements, a priori excluded from self-referential art, nonetheless continue to raise questions, and re-enter the work as reifications. The rear-view mirror is yet another symbol of self-referentiality, of constantly looking back towards the act of painting. As for the flashlight, it can now be said to belong to Johns' vocabulary of objects.

Watchman, painted that same year, in a still more vigorous style, has a chair and artificial leg inserted in the upper right-hand corner. This synedoche for the body allows us to imagine a man, suspended in air, watching. A chromatic field is surrounded by large shaded areas, and there is a horizontal bar at the very bottom that may be the ocean, or simply water. Will the watchman fall into the water like the diver?

Beyond the obvious richness of this composition, Johns seems to take pleasure in purposefully creating enigmas.

He overcomes this tendency in *According to What* (Fig. 48), a large painting, sixteen feet wide. This time the added object plays only an accessory role. The paint is spread out, as is often the case, in large vertical sections, the words "Red," "Yellow" and "Blue" are written out in such a way that they mirror one another; there is a row of colored circles; and finally, on the right-hand side, a streak of blue against a red and yellow background with a newspaper collage placed on the diagonal. Each of these sections, a remarkable painting in and of itself, work together harmoniously. After seeing them together one can easily imagine them separately, another sign of Johns' talent.

There are other elements of the artist's mythology in this painting that should not go unnoticed.

The painting can be seen as a catalogue — or repertoire — of the painter's main motifs. It includes an anatomical fragment, a broken and glued chair, a turned around canvas stretcher with an inscription, a twisted coat hanger, letters, the spectrum of grey and hinges... In short, everything that can be found in his other large compositions is included in this work. Johns is no doubt the only artist of his generation who has suceeded in realising a global synthesis of all his past work, which only adds to their value. But "according to what" do these different elements go together? This work has been considered by some to be a response to Duchamp's *Tu m'*..., pointed in 1918 and on display at the Art Gallery of Yale University. This interpretation seems to be a rather loose one and, no matter what Johns' devotion to Duchamp was during that period, the similarities between the two paintings are vague, if not completely hidden.

Oh yes, there is one common point. *Tu m'*..., was Duchamp's last painting and *According to What* is painted as though it were Johns' last painting — a sort of pictorial will.

Out of all the major works produced from 1964 on, I readily pair *Studio* and *Out of the Window*, even if one was painted quite a bit earlier than the other, because they both illustrate Johns' fascination for light and transparency. According to his friends, the first thing that he did when he moved into a new studio, was replace the old glass panes with picture windows. Light, which we can perceive in so many of his paintings, has always been important to him and is unquestionably one of his inspirations.

We can already find transparency, accentuated by color, in the work from 1962, in the large white rectangles tipped over in *Studio I* or standing upright in *Eddingsville* (Fig. 50) and *Studio II* (Fig. 52) as well as in an *Untitled* (Fig. 49) painting from 1964-1965, acquired by the Municiple Museum of Amsterdam. These works are entirely devoted to the study light and transparency. The same can be said for the right section of *Harlem Light* (Fig. 57) which resembles a crooked window, opaque under layers of dust, spotted with blue dots.

We should also add *Screen Pieces* (Fig. 59) from 1968, which stands out not only because of the inserted object, in this case a fork, but because of its treatment of light.

Along with light, Johns was also inspired by sound: voice and music. We will briefly mention an aspect of his creation that will not be developed in any lenght here: his sets and artistic direction for Merce Cunningham's dance company, who performed to John Cage's music, the dancer as well as the composer being a close friend of Johns'. This digression is intended to help clarify some of the large works that mark important stages in the painter's development. I am thinking in particular about *Voice I* and *Voice II* (Fig. 62). The letters of the word "VOICE 2," painted in muted tones of grey, blue and green, are superimposed on top of one another and become entangled, a little like the notes of a musical score

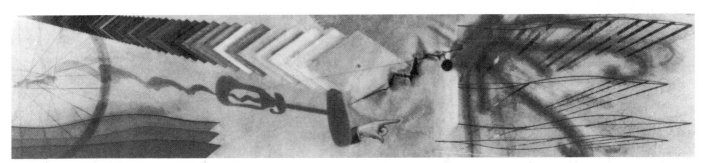

Marcel Duchamp: *Tu m'*. 1918.
Oil and pencil on canvas, 27½ × 123¼ in. (69,8 × 313 cm).

on a staff. While the work has always been displayed flat against the wall, it was designed by Johns so that it could be rearranged to form a cylinder. Because of this, it has the possibility of being viewed in three different ways, depending on the spectator's position. Various combinations are possible: A B C or B C A or C B A, just like certain musical motifs, such as the canons. The same can be said about the numbers. It has occured to me that the first act of Robert Wilson's *Einstein on the Beach* and the repetitive rythmic score of Philip Glass's *One, Two, Three, Four* might have been inspired by Jasper Johns or constitute some kind of a homage to his work. Music adds another dimension to simple signs, and in retrospect the paintings can appear as musical scores. Such is the suggestive power of numbers, especially when they are drummed out by the dance steps of Lucinda Childs.

In *Decoy* (Fig. 67), another important work painted one year after *Voice II*, Johns brings together many of his familiar motifs: the hanging leg, like the one in *Watchman*; the names of colors; an image of an ale can; and on the bottom, arranged as a predella, an image of his first sculptures.

In this particular instance, it is possible that the lithograph was done before the painting. However, since the painter is continually reusing the same motifs, it is difficult to establish an exact chronology, except for those works that were dated with precision. The last work from this first period — or rather, this period of growth, of taking a stance, of composing a register of themes — is a decorative work. It is a *Map* (Fig. 61) that was designed and produced for the World's Fair Expo of 1967 in Montreal. This *Map* has nothing in common with his earlier *Map*'s (Fig. 46) in which the names of the states and their shapes serve as the subject matter for large chromatic symphonies. This time, Johns takes Buckminster Fuller's Dymaxion Air Ocean World as his subject matter and reproduces it in his own style on a scale that is more than thirty feet wide and fifteen feet tall. The work disintegrates into a multitude of contiguous triangles, a method of triangulation destined to compensate for the earth's curvature which is not an aesthetic innovation, but an enactment of a method designed by geographer Buckminster Fuller's, known above all for his geodesic domes, made from assembled triangles. Fuller's style can certainly be detected in Johns' work.

From 1967 on, the *Flagstones* and the *Turtle Shells* occupy an important position. The names of these works obviously refer to forms that appear in a series of paintings. Johns used their outlines and filled them in with colors: black, red etc.

Is it possible to talk about "periods" in Johns' work? The term is inappropriate because Johns does not move from one theme to the next, but accumulates them and mixes them together, often in unpredictable ways, as we have already seen with his *Flag, Target, Letter,* and *Number* paintings. However, these overlapping parallelepiped forms can be said to constitute a genuinely new contribution to the painter's style.

As he often does, Johns explained the introduction of these new forms in his paintings with an anecdote, as though he wanted to deny the possibility of coming up with an idea on his own. This time, the scene is Harlem, on a highway leading to the airport. According to Michael Crichton he saw either a car, or a wall painted to look like flagstones. He wanted to take a picture of it but could not find his camera. More than their colors, he retained in particular the arrangement of the flagstones, the way in which they were assembled, like those walls made from piling up various sized stones that have existed since antiquity under the name of *opus incertum*. He put this system of assembly to work in a painting which he began a little later called *Harlem Light* (1967, Fig. 67).

The title erases any doubt about the source of inspiration. Large black and red shapes sprawl across a chalk colored pavement. The rythm is strong and suggests mural-like properties. The shapes appear as large patches of light with glowing fires and shaded spots. This describes the left side of the large painting (sixteen feet across). The right side is painted in a style with which Johns is already familiar: a superimposition of blue, white and red squares and a large grey canvas stretcher marked with white squares and spotted with blue which spreads out from the upper part of the composition. The airy lightness of this side contrasts sharply with the massive construction of the left side. It would be a diptych if the two parts were equal, but a somewhat neutral zone separates the two, creating a dichotomy instead, as though the artist wanted to depict two sides of the same reality.

Johns will frequently use this new motif. We find it in *Wall Piece,* for example, painted in 1969; and then again in a large-scale composition that is in the Ludwig Museum in Cologne. The entire middle panel of the piece is covered by flagstones and separates a panel of crosshatching on the left from an assembly of pieces of raw wood on the right.

A new style

In 1972 a new period began with the *crosshatchings*. Just what are these crosshatchings? A visual method that appeals to drawing, gesture and color, it animates the surface without totally covering it. And in the hands of Johns this method becomes an effective style. Beneath a haphazard appearance, the stripes are painted in a rigorous order we will attempt to decipher.

The idea for these colored signs may have come to him after seeing a Mexican barber shop sign painted on a tree. The sign was made up of stongly colored woven stripes which resembled a man's beard. This is only a hypothesis. More likely, they are simply decorative and/or symbolic motifs. But a potentially effective system, contained within the barber's unpretentious and colorful sign, immediately appealed to Johns who would later experiment with it and develop it.

A less poetic source has been suggested by Michael Crichton who says that Jasper Johns discovered these signs in *National Geographic*, number 143, page 668, to be exact. Once again, what difference does it make? Only the painting itself matters.

These grids are difficult to decipher, and many viewers are satisfied by the simple visual pleasure they receive from their rythm and color. The titles that seem to offer a clue as to what they might mean, do not always reveal as much as we would like them to. At times they seem to be alluding to figurative forms, but how can we be sure? They often recall the compositions of a well known painter whose work has been an inspiration to Johns. The hatchings accentuate the surface much as the meter does in a poem by Horace. But the diversity of each verse, or in the case of Johns, each group of parallel hatchings, results in harmony, which is not to say a general uniformity of the whole.

Certain works are broken up into large masses of different colorations that are flamboyantly energetic. Other masses stand out because they are nearly monochrome, usually in muted colors, such as brown or violet. They are compelling especially because of their density, which demonstrates the painter's determination to push an idea to its extreme, an idea so simple that it could not be false.

At the heart of his system is an obsessive pursuit of all possible intersecting angles within a spectrum of limited colors. Johns creates symmetrical patterns between the top and bottom and between the left and right panels, as though the different parts of the works are mirroring each other.

Johns could not let the hatchings proliferate in an uncontrolled continuum without falling into the very type of abstraction he rejects. This is comparable to how Dubuffet proceeded in *L'hourloupe*. He let the signs, which were almost always the same except for several close variations, invade the surface. The result is not only decorative, it is meaningful. Like the flags and concentric circles of the targets, which throughout his career have served as frameworks on which he can experiment with pictorial variations, Johns will use simple frameworks on which to develop his crosshatches, frameworks that often give the painting its title.

Richard Francis supports this point when he writes: "Johns established rules for the directions and colors of his brushstrokes in the first painting and adhered to them."[7] This consistency can be found much later on, as recently as 1980, in *Dancer on a Plane*, now on display at the Tate Gallery in London.

Thus we can see how Johns, in his development of a single and apparently simple technique, continually renews his work.

---

7. See *Johns*, New York: Abbeville Press, 1984.

Pablo Picasso: *Weeping Woman*. 1937.
Oil on canvas, 23½ × 19¼ in. (60 × 49 cm).

Edvard Munch: *Self-portrait Between the Clock and the Bed*. 1940-1942.
Oil on canvas 59 × 47¼ in. (150 × 120 cm).

The first major work to use crosshatches is called *Scent* (Fig. 74), painted in 1973-74 as a homage to Jackson Pollock, the title taken from one of his paintings.

At first glance, the composition seems to be strictly organized according to a horizontal rhythm of red stripes that dominate over the less numerous green, blue and black ones. A closer look, however, reveals a triptych made from three juxtaposed paintings, each one done separately since they do not exactly fit together as usual. The longer the eye lingers, the more the red and green stripes stand out in their luminosity, bearing a certain resemblance to a musical score. This sense of musicality is undoubtedly where the link to Jackson Pollock lies. Perhaps *Scent* should be viewed as a rigorously controlled dripping, or an image of a dripping, from now on a technique that belongs to the formal vocabulary of painting.

The musical and chromatic *Corpse and Mirror* compositions came next, made entirely from the assemblage of painted canvases that can be seen separately or, when the continuity between the diverse elements corresponds, side by side. Strangely enough, *The Barber's Tree* (Fig. 72), which inspired this style in 1972, does not appear as the title of a painting until 1975. It is a densely painted work with an entangled grid that resembles a thick beard, and over time, looks less like a sign than a mural painting with all its decorative qualities.

The crosshatchings are both a style and a method which Johns developed and continues to use. They can be found in his major works, such as *Dutch Wives*, a diptych made up of two vertical portraits. Through the hatches, a kind of classical Flemish portrait from the seventeenth century can be detected perhaps by Rubens, Frans Hals or Rembrandt, in particular because of their dark tones. In *Weeping Women* (Fig. 71) from that same year (1975), a decidedly productive time, we can make out the outline of Picasso's *Femmes qui Pleurent*. Three different versions of this work exist, all from 1937, one predominantly red, the other predominantly ochre, the third in blue, as though he was presenting declensions of the same motif, which is undoubtedly the case.

The series of these powerful paintings is a long one, and includes *Céline* from 1978, a painting that blends crosshatches in the upper part with flagstones in the lower part; the sparkling *Cicada*; and finally, *Between the Clock and the Bed* (Fig. 88).

Later on, these styles will no longer be used alone, but mixed with others in complex and multi-styled compositions.

The two versions of *Between the Clock and the Bed*, painted in 1981 and 1982-83, are not only remarkable compositions, but also obvious demonstrations of Jasper Johns' method. His very first use of crosshatchings preceeds these works by ten years, dating back to 1972 to be exact, when they appeared in an *Untitled* painting (Fig. 66).

In considering Johns' original crosshatching style, one can understand his astonishment when he found himself face to face with a perfect specimen of crosshatching, done thirty years before by an old Norwegian painter. Edvard Munch is the greatest Norwegian painter of the century and one of the most important in the world history of painting. He has influenced several generations of painters with the expressive, violent and powerful style that made him one of the precursors of Expressionism. Even Picasso was influenced by him in the first part of the twentieth century. In the famous painting, *Between the Clock and the Bed*, the objects represented are not merely pieces of furniture but symbols between which Munch places his full self-portrait. Rendered by an authentic crosshatching technique, the bedspread, which may be a patchwork and is in any case a folk inspired material (one thinks of Lapp art), is slightly coarse, primitive and violent. Although we would usually view this image with an indifferent eye, we see it in a new light having become acquainted with Johns' work.

We can only imagine the shock that Johns must have felt on seeing Munch's painting during a large museum exhibition. But we know for sure what the consequences of his reaction were, since he painted two *Between the Clock and the Beds* in 1981, and another one the following years.

In the first one he re-employs the distribution of colored masses: the left side has brown and violet hatchings, the colors of the clock, the jacket and the figure; the center is orange and the central fireplace a luminous yellow; the right side has a greenish door and a painted figure; and finally, in the lower right-hand corner, the red of the bedspread treated in a completely different way. It is here that Johns demonstrates his independence and creative spirit: he is inspired by his model, but refuses to copy and offers us a work that is of a profoundly different nature.

The graphics

In order to fully appreciate Johns' contribution to contemporary art, it is necessary to take all of his work into account, not only the paintings that are hanging in the museums and important collections, but also the drawings and prints. His drawings are not merely preparatory studies, but works in and of themselves, artistic investigations carried out at the same time as the painted work but in a different medium.

The prints — lithographs and etchings — were originally done in order to enlarge the audience of this already well known artist whose rapidly rising prices excluded the small and medium range collectors.

Although Jasper Johns uses the same motifs again and again, he is incapable of doing the same painting more than once. Also, his lithographs of the flags, targets, numbers and letters in no way resemble reproductions. First of all, the technique is completely different and limits him to transpositions, variations and adaptations. Secondly, Johns fully exploits and delights in the medium's specificities, and the work that comes off the stone or zinc plate is entirely original. Collectors value these infinite variations as new alternatives to the painted work, and they prove just as rich in a sensitivity that is revealed in many different ways.

Jasper Johns has claimed that he does not like to draw, but he is nonetheless a passionate drawer who handles the pencil with a fervor that sometimes borders on frenzy. His 1955 drawings of flags and targets provide us with a good example of this. The motifs appear and disappear beneath shading drawn in jerky gestures, giving the impression of a texture and transparency comparable to that of oils. The motifs used are a mere pretext by which to illustrate the possibilities, the richness and the spendor of graphite lead. In his fervor Johns does not, however, sacrifice precision: the lines are straight, the circles round, and the stars clearly drawn. He sometimes goes so far as to precisely draw a diagram of the construction for the cans which will be cast. In this particular instance the drawing is a plan for a work yet to come.

While Johns reacted against the omnipresence of Abstract Expressionism, he did not reject its lesson and, in the manner of certain Surrealists and literary models (Breton had been in New York), he adopted an equivalent to automatic writing which lends a poetic quality to his graphic and pictorial technique. We can even detect a certain gesturality in the drawings of this extremely controlled painter. But unlike the masters of Action Painting, Johns maintains a distanced, objectified and controlled gesturality. It does not explode outside of the frame's limits, as it does with Franz Kline for example, but remains imprisoned, somewhat cramped, within the confines of the motif that serves as its framework. Jasper Johns only gave into his gestural impulses within the strict limitations that he imposed. The prints did not begin until several years after the drawings when, in 1960, he met the directors of ULAE (Universal Limited Art Editions) in West Islip, a small town on Long Island, New York. Tatiana Grosman, the director of the lithography workshop, offered him his first stone. He experimented with it, developed a taste for it and discovered lithography's endless possibilities. After his first *Target*, Johns produced more than one hundred and fifty prints at ULAE between 1960 and 1979.

Johns' printed work is known to us largely through several catalogue essays, written with extreme care and competence, for major exhibitions.

First of all, there is the essay by Riva Castelman written for the retrospective of prints at the Museum of Modern Art in 1986. It should be noted that MOMA owns one of the most important collections of contemporary prints in the world. An earlier work by Christian Geelhaar should also be mentioned. This significant study was published at the Museum of Basle for *Working Proofs*, a very successful exhibition that travelled to Munich, London and Barcelona. The two volumes are made up of interviews with the artist, who shares his ideas on this particular form of expression. Geelhaar has also published a table that lists Johns' production, year by year, and by publisher.

In a period of twenty years, between 1960 and 1979, Johns made two hundred and eighty prints, of which one hundred and eighty-five are lithographs, seventy-eight are etchings, and only seventeen are silk-screens. The majority were produced and printed at ULAE and Gemini, except for the etchings, which for the most part were done in Paris at Crommelynck.

The *Working Proofs* exhibition gave us the opportunity to get an inside view of Johns' creative process. They expose his trials and errors, his will to achieve perfection or at least the perfect realization of his will, and an extraordinary professional consciousness.

Johns' comments and various accounts reveal an artist who is frustrated by the fact that he cannot completely control the finished product. He works and reworks the stone or metal plate as many times as he needs to in order to produce a working proof that satisfies him. Johns tends to be more temperamental during the printing phase, since slight variations in colors, for example, can become exasperating problems. If Jasper Johns is recognized today as one of the best lithographers alive, his prints and etchings attaining exceptionally high prices, it is without a doubt due to the quality of his work, and to the quality of his printing technique.

We have already mentioned the infinite variations that the stone permits the artist to develop of his favorite motifs, something we can witness from his very first *Target*, which in this case resembles an eye that stares back at us. But we should also add that the technique prompted Johns to discover new possibilities and to develop different themes.

While Johns used photography in *Souvenir* (of Japan) from 1970, for example, or in order to make the image of the Mona Lisa appear in the curve of a number, he used lithography for the *Skins*. Beginning with a print of his hand, he then multiplied it into hallucinating compositions, and later went on to reproduce other fragments of skin, such as his own body and feet. His lithography experience also proved advantageous to him later on when he illustrated Samuel Beckett's *Fizzles/Foirades*.

It is facinating to follow the process, step by step, from painting to lithograph. For example, taking a painting from 1964, *According to What* (Fig. 48), or rather a detail from the painting, in this case an inserted canvas stretcher, he then transcribed it to a lithographic stone in two dimensions. He made several different attempts. In the first version he drew the object in shades of grey; in the next he made a line drawing; then he gave the illusion of volume by applying a uniform shading; and finally he toned down the transcription of the other colored parts in order to give a homogeneity to the print. The technical process is a remarkable one in which Johns seems to hesitate and multiply his attempts before making up his mind.

He produced this image in 1971, seven years after the painting. In another important work from 1971, a particularly productive year, he started from *Untitled*, a 1963 gouache with collage that has the Coca Cola logo in it. From this painting, he created a new work similar to the first one, which he then transformed into a sort of mirror image. In the final version only the most essential elements are left, those which attribute the work its power: the logo, one letter, a hand print, and the outline of a brush, all on a grid of lined paper.

Johns always takes margins into account, and even when his prints are framed, they are surrounded by a border of blank paper. He is also preoccupied with the scale of the prints. When he continues from a painting in order to draw on the stone, he does not enlarge or reduce indiscriminately. As far as Johns is concerned, no detail is too small.

At the end of a long interview he offers the following comments about his printing technique: ''What you say about my tendency to add things is correct. But how does one make a painting? How does one deal with the space? Does one have something and then proceed to add another thing or does one have one something; move into it; occupy it; divide it; make the best one can of it? I think I do different things at different times and perhaps at the same time. I find it interesting that a part can function as a whole or that a whole can be thrown into a situation in which it is only a part. It interests me that what one takes to be a whole subject can suddenly be miniaturized, or something, and then inserted into another world, as it were.''

Johns had the opportunity to put these concepts into action thanks to a meeting with a very private man, a master who plays with words, the provocative playwright, Samuel Beckett. There are definite affinities between these two artists. Paradoxes, the unnameable and plays on words (inherited from Joyce), correspond with Johns' motifs. He devoted many months of relentless work to this project at the Crommelynck Brothers' workshop. The result is neither painting nor printing, but a book, and what a book it is! It is impossible to describe for it contains all of Johns. As for Beckett: ''To name, no, nothing is nameable, to say, no, nothing is sayable.''

The *Four Seasons*

The Venice Biennale 1988: the international art world casts a powerful beam of light on Jasper Johns and his work. His position as one of the greatest contemporary painters — something the whole world already knew — is confirmed. And this kind of public triumph should not be dismissed as inconsequential. It confirms the judgement of the experts and the market which has made him the most expensive living painter in the world today. In the spring of 1988 a major work, and admittedly a large one, sold at Christies in New York for more than five million dollars.

The cosmopolitan crowd that converged in Venice filed past the *Four Seasons* in the Giardini, much like the Japanese did in front of the *Mona Lisa* twenty-five years ago. The work is not questioned, but honored, and only the most naive try to penetrate the secret of his artistic creation and interpret a message. This large and most recent work certainly deserves the attention. The *Four Seasons*, painted in 1986, appear to us a kind of synthesis into which Johns has poured all of his knowledge, all of his talent and all of his ideas about art and man.

And, for the first time he portrays himself, in the form of a life-size human shadow. As with much of Johns' work, *The Four Seasons* is a genuine puzzle. The work is loaded with references of all kinds, possibly to Duchamp, Dada or even Mathias Grünewald whose religious compositions have supposedly affected and impressed the artist, if we are to believe Jill Johnston who developed this interpretation in a long article in the magazine *Art in America*. This analysis, unsettling in its subtlety, is only valid if it receives an approval or consent from the creator himself, even a reticent one. Art critics today practice philosophy, psychoanalysis and even history, proving that we can only adapt to a civilization that insists on mediation. But nothing will prevent writers of all kinds from giving free rein to their imaginations and coming up with the most improbable interpretations and the least obvious associations. Not everyone can be André Malraux or Élie Faure.

Contrary to what certain European observers may say or write, the appearance of these tall figures does not in any way constitute a return to figuration, and the evolution of Jasper Johns' work has nothing to do with that of the German or Italian Transavantguardia. The *Four Seasons* (Figs. 97 to 100) belong instead to the spirit of a traditional teme — ''the stages of life'' — often depicted in popular art, in Epinal images, in which one sees a baby, a boy, a young man climbing a stairway, a mature man standing on top, and finally, an old man climbing down the stairs towards death.

Like everyone else, Johns is also preoccupied with aging and his work takes on a symbolic value here. He seems to be taking stock of the situation and looks both to the past and to the future.

The silhouette of the man does not change from one season to the next. The outline of the painter's shadow was traced by his friend Julien Lethbridge only once and has been reproduced on each panel. Its position, however, does change; it is in the center in *Spring* (Fig. 97), to the left in *Summer* (Fig. 98), cut in two with half on the left and half on the right in *Fall* (Fig. 99) — the season that corresponds to Johns' age when he painted the work, and to the far right in *Winter* (Fig. 100), which ends the cycle.

The passage of time is inscribed on a sort of clock. It recalls the semicircles of *Device*, which are also positioned vertically. In *Spring*, the hand is raised towards the top, and an arrow pointing to the left, counter clockwise, conveys a sense of movement. In *Summer*, the hand is horizontal, in *Fall* it is at eight o'clock, and in *Winter* it points downwards, but the arrow which in all the other seasons points counter-clockwise, is in this last panel pointing clockwise, and seems to be confining the hand to the bottom. The symbolism here is obvious. The other images in the quadriptych, mostly quotations from his past work, are less symbolic. It should also be noted that the four panels were not painted in the order of the seasons. The first, *Summer*, was painted in 1985 and the three others in 1986.

Up until this time, Johns devoted himself to compositions whose various elements will show up later in the *Four Seasons*. Among these works are *In the Studio* (Fig. 85) and *Perilous Night* from 1982, and then several *Untitled* (Fig. 87) works from 1983 that include the inscriptions "Chutes de glace" in French and "Gletscherrabbfall" in German. In 1984 there are several wide compositions made from collages of images that look like reproductions taped to the wall, with the added inscriptions "foot," "knee" and "face," and a Toulouse-Lautrec reproduction. That same year he made *Racing Thoughts* (Fig. 96) which uses a similar process of juxtaposed images, the *Mona Lisa* (a homage to Duchamp), the inscription "Chute de glace," and a portrait and a painting in crosshatching.

All of the elements from these rather calm works, painted between 1982 and 1984, reappear in the *Four Seasons*. But this time a new element is added — his silhouette. And if the evolution of the work is considered in terms of style, it is no less a new element. The artist, who has always hidden his feelings beneath objects that are apparently meaningless on the psychological level, now portrays himself. He has claimed that he does not want his work to reveal his feelings: "In my early work, I tried to hide my personality, my psychological state, my emotions. This was party due to my feelings about painting at the time. I sort of stuck to my guns for a while but eventually it seemed like a losing battle. Finally one must simply drop the reserve. I think some of the changes in my work relate to that."

So then, can we consider *Savarin* (Fig. 78) to be a self-portrait? Of course we can, even if he limited himself to depicting the tools of his trade.

From 1985 on, Jasper Johns no longer hides himself but is present in the work. His silhouette leans slightly, as though he were trying to thrust himself forward, almost to the point of falling. The shadow dominates the work and is its center; the symbols with which he surrounds the shadow seem to determine its destiny.

In the first panel, *Summer*, many of his favorite motifs are depicted: stars (but are they the stars of the American flag or do they belong to the night sky above the seahorse?); a ladder, from which a painting hangs by a rope, a painting done in crosshatchings that appropriates a section of Isenheim de Mathias Grünewald's altarpieces; the *Mona Lisa*; two flags; pots from his collection of pottery by George Ohr, a ceramicist from the beginning of the century; and other more or less recognizable elements. In short, Johns portrays himself in the prime of his life, surrounded by those elements which have made him so famous. *Summer* is the most powerful panel, or in any case, the most colorful. In the other panels, different motifs are presented. In *Spring*, his silhouette is cut off at the knees by that of a child who is framed in a rectangle and covered by an abstract drawing made up of two squares, two triangles and two circles. Strange antique-looking vases create the profiles of Queen Elizabeth and Prince Philip in negative. In *Fall*, everything has shattered: the man's body is cut in two, the ladder is broken and the paintings are falling down. But at the top of the painting the same two squares, two triangles and two circles that make their way into each of the four panels appear intact. *Winter* brings back the calm and everything finds its place once again, on a watered-down bluish grey surface obscured beneath the white flurries of a snowfall.

Each of the seasons has a colored ladder, in red and white or green and black, like some mysterious instrument.

Beginning in 1980, Jasper Johns turned to past works for material. He has claimed that old art is a critique of new art, and vice versa. However, it is only with difficul-

Pablo Picasso: *L'ombre*. 1953.
Oil and charcoal on canvas, 51 × 38 in. (129,5 × 96,5 cm).

ty that one can make the traces. In the paintings from 1982 to 1984 that we have already mentioned, the outline of the wounded warriors from Grünewald's *Resurrection* appears in the background. The *Four Seasons* bears a certain resemblance to a painting by Picasso from 1953 intitled *L'Ombre*, and also to some of Matisse's work which has used this same effect of back-lighting. The ladder's position and the hanging of the paintings in *Summer* remind us of another painting by Picasso, *Minotaure transportant sa maison*, from 1936. This bringing together of various elements creates an interesting effect. As Picasso was known to say, you have to take it where you find it, and art from the past is rich in simulations of all kinds. Already in the mid-seventies, Johns spoke of the appropriation of art history. For many young artists, art in the eighties is an art of reference, and no one hesitates to partake in the borrowing, or more precisely in the quotation, of the artists he admires, as writers have always done.

Johns in his turn practises these veiled allusions to masterpieces from the past, but so secretly that his viewer has to question them. Is he playing some kind of game in which the viewer has to guess where these mysterious signs come from? Does he prefer to hide them in order to better excite the art lover's curiosity?

The *Four Seasons* will remain a key work in the evolution of Jasper Johns. They mark a liberation of his earlier reserve. But is this not more important for him than it is for us? The ensemble is dark and impressive because it is dominated by a huge human form. But what is gained in emotion is lost in pictorial impact.

What else does the artist have in store for us?

CHRONOLOGY

1930. Jasper Johns was born in Augusta, Georgia on May 15, the son of Jasper Johns and Jean Riley Johns. He spent is childhood in Allendale, South Carolina, with his grand-parents, an aunt and an uncle after his parents separated. He went to school in Columbia and later in The Corner, a small South Carolina Community. He completed his studies in Sumter, South Carolina where he lived with his mother, step-father, his half-sisters and half-brother.

1947-48. University of South Carolina.

1949. Commercial art school in New York. Receives scholarship. Works as a clerk and then spends two years in the army, train-ing at Fort Jackson, then stationed in Japan until 1952.

1952. Spends two days at Hunter College, works at Marboro bookstore.

1954. Is introduced to Robert Rauschenberg, five years his elder, by Suzi Gablik, and then to John Cage and Morton Feldman. Along with Rauschenberg he supports himself by designing window displays for department stores, including Tiffany's. He moves from 83rd Street to 8th Street, and then to Pearl Street and to Fulton Street, where he is Rauschenberg's neighbour. He has already started drawing and making collages, but in 1954 he destroys all of his work with the exception of four pieces.

1955. First *Flag* (a white one), first *Target* and first plaster casts of the face, first *Numbers*. He attends John Cage's concerts.

1956-57. Paints his first *Alphabets* (grey) and begings to incorporate objects into his paintings in *Canvas, Book* and *Drawer*. He participates in the New York School Artists, Second Genera-tion exhibition at the Jewish Museum. First contact with Leo Castelli, and the hanging of one of his paintings in the gallery.

1958. First solo exhibition at Leo Castelli Gallery with *Flags, Targets* and *Numbers*. He will show with Castelli throughout his career, and continues to do so today. One of his paint-ings appears on the cover of the important American magazine *Art News*. Alfred Barr, director of the Museum of Modern Art in New York, buys several of his works. Johns begins to make three dimensional pieces with casts: *Light Bulb* and *Flashlight*. Along with Robert Rauschenberg, he participates in John Cage's retrospective concert at the Town Hall in New York. This same year he exhibits in the American Pavillon at the Venice Biennale.

1959. Is included in the Carnegie International and wins the Carnegie Prize. Discovers Marcel Duchamp through Robert Motherwell's book on Dada painters and poets. Sees the Duchamp exhibition at the Philadelphia Museum. Reads Robert Lebel's book on Duchamp and is brought to Duchamp's studio on Front Street by Nicolas Calas. Par-ticipation in Alan Kaprow's happening by designing part of the decor with Rauschenberg.

1960. The year of the *Ballantine Ale Cans* and the *Savarin* coffee. First lithographs at ULAE (Universal Limited Art Editions) on the invitation of Tatiana Grossman.

1961. First *Maps* of the United States. Reads Wittgenstein. Buys house in Edisto Beach, South Carolina. Performs with David Tudor for John Cage's *Variations II* in Paris along with Rauschenberg, Tinguely and Niky de Saint-Phalle. Designs costumes for Merce Cunningham's *Good Time Charley by the Sea*.

1962. Paints *Fool's House*.

1963. Rents a penthouse on Riverside Drive, New York. Works in South Carolina. Creates the Foundation for Contemporary Performance Art. Paints *Diver* and *Periscope*.

1964. First solo retrospective at the Jewish Museum with catalogue essays by John Cage and Alan Salomon. Trip to Hawaii and Japan. Paints *Watchman* Venice Biennale (where Rauschenberg wins the grand prize). Retrospective exhi-bition at the Whitechapel Gallery in London.

1965. Exhibition in Pasadena curated by Walter Hopps. Prize at the Biennale of Prints in Ljubljana, Yugoslavia.

1966. Exhibition of drawings in Washington. His home in Edisto Beach is detroyed by fire.

1967. Moves to Canal Street. First appearance of flagstone motif in *Harlem Light*. Becomes artistic director for Merce Cun-ningham. First etchings at ULAE. Wins São Paulo Biennale prize. Creates *Map* according to Buckminster Fuller's Dymaxion Air Ocean Projection of the world for the United States Pavilion at the World's Fair in Montreal.

1968. Designs costumes inspired by Duchamp's *Large Glass* for Merce Cunningham's performance in Buffalo. Works on a series of *Number* and *Letter* lithographs at Gemini in Los Angeles. His printed work will occupy an important po-sition in his life up until 1970.

1970. Retrospective of his prints curated by Richard Field at the Philadelphia Museum which then travels to the Museum of Modern Art in New York, thanks to Riva Castelman.

1972. Crosshatchings appear for the first time in a large *Untitled* painting. Skowhegan Medal for Painting. Designs costumes for Cunningham's *T. V. Rerun* and *Landrover*.

1973. Meets Samuel Beckett in Paris, whose book he will illustrate in 1975. Record price paid by Park Bernet for *Double White Map* which sold at auction for $ 240,000.

1974. Paints *Scent* in homage to Pollock.

1975. Illustrates *Fizzles/Foirades* by Samuel Beckett at the Crom-melynck workshop in Paris. Paints *The Dutch Wives* and *Weeping Women*.

1977. Retrospective exhibition at the Whitney Museum with more than two hundred works and a catalogue by Michael Crichton. The exhibition travels to Europe and Japan.

1978. Major exhibition of prints curated by Richard Field at Wesleyan University.

1979. *Working Proof* exhibition curated by Christian Geelhaar appears first at the Basle Museum and then travels throughout Europe.

1980. The Whitney Museum buys *Three Flags* for $ 1,000.000.

1981. Paints *Between the Clock and the Bed*, inspired by Edvard Munch.

1982. New prints at ULAE.

1985-86. After many studies, paints the *Four Seasons*.

1987. Leo Castelli exhibits the *Four Seasons* in his gallery on West Broadway.

1988. The *Four Seasons* win the grand prize at the Venice Biennale.

BIBLIOGRAPHY

General works

Baigell, Matthieu. *A History of American Painting*, London: Thames and Hudson, 1971.

Battcock, Gregory. *The New Art*, New York: Dutton & Co., 1966.

Lippard, Lucy. *Pop'Art*, London: Thames and Hudson, 1966.

Lippard, Lucy. *Le Pop-Art*, Paris: Nathan, 1969.

Pleynet, Marcelin. *Les États-Unis de la peinture*, Paris: Éd. du Seuil, 1986.

Pluchard, François. *Pop'Art et Cie*, Paris: Martin-Malburet, 1971.

Rose, Barbara. *American Art since 1900:* A Critical History, London: Thames and Hudson, 1967; Brussels: Éd. de la Connaissance, 1964.

Rosenberg, Harold. *The Anxious Object. Art Today and its Audience.* New York: The Horizon Press, 1964.

[Several Authors]. *Peinture Américaine*, Paris: Galilée/Art Press, 1980.

Monographs

Alloway, Lawrence. «Jasper Johns and Robert Rauschenberg», in: *Figurative Art since 1945*, London: Thames and Hudson, 1971.

Castelman, Riva. *A Print Retrospective*, New York: Museum of Modern Art, 1986.

Calas, Elena and Nicola. «Jasper Johns: And Or», in: *Icons + Images of the Sixties*, New York: Dutton, Toronto: Clarke, Irving & Co., 1971, p. 72-82.

Crichton, Michael. *Jasper Johns*, New York: Abrams, 1977.

Francis, Richard. *Jasper Johns*, New York: Abbeville Press, 1984.

Geelhaar, Christian. *Jasper Johns Working Proofs*, London: Petersburg Press, 1976.

Kozloff, Max. *Jasper Johns*, New York: Abrams, n.d. [1967?]; republished in 1974.

Shapiro, David. *Jasper Johns Drawings*, New York: Abrams, 1984.

Steinberg, Leo. *Jasper Johns*, New York: Wittenborn, 1963.

Main exhibitions catalogs

Cage, John. «Jasper Johns: Stories and Ideas», in: *Jasper Johns*, exhibition catalog, The Jewish Museum, New York, 1964, pp. 21-26; republished: *Jasper Johns*, exhibition catalog, Whitechapel Gallery, London, 1964, pp. 26-35; republished: John Cage, *A Year from Monday: New Lectures and Writings*, Middletown, Conn.: Wesleyan University Press, 1969, pp. 73-84.

Castelman, Riva. [Preface], in: *Jasper Johns: Lithographs*, exhibition catalog, Museum of Modern Art, New York, 1970.

Crichton, Michael. *Jasper Johns*, exhibition catalog, Harry N. Abrams and Whiney Museum of American Art, New York, 1977.

Ellin, Everett. [Preface], in: *Jasper Johns Retrospective Exhibition*, exhibition catalog, Everett Ellin Gallery, Los Angeles, 1962.

Field, Richards. *Jasper Johns: Prints 1970-1977*, London: Petersburg Press/Middletown, Conn.: Weslayan University, 1978.

Goldman, Judith. [Preface], in: *Foirades/Fizzles*, exhibition catalog, Whitney Museum of American Art, 1977. Five fragments written by Samuel Beckett and thirty-three etchings by Jasper Johns.

Hopkins, Henry. [Preface], in: *Jasper Johns: Figures 0 to 9*, engraving catalog, Gemini GEL, Los Angeles, 1968.

Hopps, Walter. [Preface], in: *Jasper Johns: Fragments-According to What*, engravings catalog, Gemini GEL, Los Angeles, 1971.

Hulten, Pontus; Robbe-Grillet, Alain; Restany, Pierre. «Jasper Johns», exhibition catalog Centre Georges Pompidou, Paris, 1978.

Musing, Stefan. [Preface], in: *The Drawings of Jasper Johns*, exhibition catalog, National Collection of Fine Arts, Washington, D.C., 1966.

Robertson, Bryan. *Jasper Johns*, exhibition catalog, Hayward Gallery, London, 1978.

Rosenblum, Robert. [Preface], in: *Jasper Johns 1955-1960*, exhibition catalog, Columbia Museum of Art, Columbia, SC, 1960.

Stanislawski, Ryszard. *Jasper Johns litografie*, exhibition catalog, Museum Sztuki w Lodzi, Lodz, 1970.

R. Solomon, Alan. *Jasper Johns*, exhibition catalog, Jewish Museum, New York, 1964. With an essay by John Cage: «Jasper Johns: Stories and Ideas».

Sylvester, David. *Jasper Johns Drawings*, exhibition catalog, Arts Council of Great Britain, London, 1974. With an interview by David Sylvester.

Selected studies in international art journals

Since these are very numerous, only a few have been chosen here, by virtue of their exceptional interest.

Alloway, Lawrence. «The Man Who Liked Cats: The Evolution of Jasper Johns», *Arts Magazine* (New York), vol. 44, no. 1, Sept-Oct. 1969, pp. 40-43. (a review by: Max Kozloff, *Jasper Johns*, New York: Abrams, 1969.)

Cage, John. «Jasper Johns: Stories and Ideas», *Art and Artists* (London), no. 3 May 1968, pp. 36-41. Extract from *A Year from Monday: Lectures and Writings by John Cage*, London: Calder and Boyars, 1967. American edition, Middletown, Conn.: Wesleyan University Press, 1969, pp. 73-84.

Francis, Richard. «Disclosures», *Art in America* (New York), vol. 72, no. 8, Sept. 1984, pp. 196-202.

Greenberg, Clement. «After Abstract Expressionism», *Art International* (Zurich), no. 6, 25 October 1962, pp. 24-32. Reviewed and republished in: Henry Geldzahler, *New York: Painting and Sculpture 1940-1970*, New York: Dutton / Metropolitan Museum of Art, 1969, pp. 360-371.

Hermann, Rolf-Dieter. «Johns the Pessimist», *Artforum* (New York), vol. 16, no. 2, Oct. 1977, pp. 26-33.

Hopps, Walter. «An Interview with Jasper Johns», *Artforum* (New York), vol. 3, no. 6, March 1965, pp. 32-36.

Kuspit, Donald B. «Personal Signs: Jasper Johns», *Art in America* (New York), vol. 69, no. 6, summer 1981, pp. 111-113.

Rose, Barbara. «The Graphic Work of Jasper Johns: Part 1», *Art forum* (New York), vol. 8, March 1970, pp. 39-45. «Part 2», *Art forum* (New York), vol. 8, Sept. 1970, pp. 65-74.

«Decoys and Doubles: Jasper Johns and the Modernist Mind», *Arts Magazine* (New York), vol. 50, May 1976, pp. 68-73.

«Jasper Johns: Pictures and Concepts», *Arts Magazine* (New York), vol. 52, nov. 1977, pp. 148-53.

Rosenberg, Harold. «Jasper Johns: Things the Mind Already Knows», *Vogue* (New York), vol. 143, February 1964, pp. 175-177, 201-203. Republished in: Harold Rosenberg, *The Anxious Object. Art Today and its Audience*, New York: The Horizon Press, 1973, pp. 176-184.

«The Art World: Twenty Years of Jasper Johns», *The New Yorker* (New York), vol. 53, Dec. 1977, pp. 42-45.

Russell, John. «Jasper Johns», *Connaissance des Arts* (Neuilly-sur-Seine), vol. 223, July 1971, pp. 48-53.

Yau, John. «Jasper Johns», *Artforum* (New York), vol. 24, no. 4, Dec. 1985, pp. 80-84.

Films

Blackwood, Michael, director and producer. *Jasper Johns*: Decoy. 1972. 18 min. (The artist working lithography. *Decoy* at ULAE).

Martin, Katrina, director and producer. *Hanafuda/Jasper Johns*. 1980. 33 min. (The artist working on serigraphs at Simca Print Artists.)

Solomon, Alan R., director, and Lane Slade, producer. *Artist No. 8: Jasper Johns*. 1966. 28 min. (Interviews with the artist and with Leo Castelli.)

ILLUSTRATIONS

1. *Untitled.* 1954.
   Painted wood, plaster and collage,
   26 × 8 in. (66 × 20.3 cm).
   Hirshhorn Museum and Sculpture Garde
   Washington D.C.

2. *Target with Four Faces.* 1955.
   Encaustic on newspaper over canvas,
   33⅝ × 26 × 3¾ in. (85.3 × 66 × 7.6 cm).
   The Museum of Modern Art, New York.
   Gift of Mr. and Mrs. Robert C. Scull.

3. *Target with Plaster Casts.* 1955.
   Encaustic and collage on canvas
   with plaster casts,
   51 × 44 × 3½ in. (129.5 × 111.7 × 9 cm).
   Mr. Leo Castelli Collection.

4. *Green Target*. 1955.
   Encaustic on newspaper over canvas,
   60×60 in. (152.4×152.4 cm).
   The Museum of Modern Art, New York.
   Richard S. Zeisler, Fund.

5. *White Flag.* 1955.
    Encaustic and collage on canvas,
    78 × 119½ in. (198 × 303 cm).
    The artist's collection.

6

7

6. *Flag*. 1955.
    Encaustic, oil and collage on canvas,
    42½ × 60⅝ in. (107.3 × 153.8 cm).
    The Museum of Modern Art, New York.
    Gift of Philip Johnson in honor
    of Alfred H. Barr, Jr.

7. *Tango*. 1955.
    Encaustic and collage on canvas with objects,
    43 × 55 in. (109.2 × 139.7 cm).
    Private collection.

8. *Canvas*. 1956.
    Encaustic on canvas over wood,
    30 × 25 in. (76.2 × 63.5 cm).
    The artist's collection.

9. *Drawer*. 1957.
    Encaustic and assemblage on canvas,
    30¾ × 30¾ in. (78 × 78 cm).
    Rose Art Museum, Brandeis University,
    Waltham, Ma.
    Gevirtz-Mnuchin Purchase Fund.

8

9

10. *Flag on Orange Field*. 1957.
Encaustic on canvas,
66 × 49 in. (167.6 × 124.5 cm).
Museum Ludwig, Cologne.

11. *Book*. 1957.
Encaustic on book,
10 × 13 in. (25.4 × 33 cm).
Anne and Martin Z. Margulies
Collection, Miami, Fla.

12. *Numbers in Color*. 1958-1959.
Encaustic and collage on canvas,
67 × 49½ in. (170 × 126 cm).
Albright-Knox Art Gallery, Buffalo.

13. *Target*. 1958.
Pencil, wash and collage on paper
mounted on cardboard,
14⅞ × 13⅞ in. (38 × 35.5 cm).
Modern Art Museum of Forth Worth.
The Benjamin J. Tillar Memorial Trust.

14. *Black Numbers*. 1958.
Crayon on paper,
30½ × 24 in. (77.5 × 61 cm).
Ohara Museum of Art, Kurashiki.

10

11

12

13

14

15. *Three Flags.* 1958.
Encaustic on canvas,
30⅛ × 45½ × 5 in. (76.5 × 116 × 12.7 cm).
The Whitney Museum of American Art,
50th Anniversary Gift of The Gilman Foundation, Inc.,
The Lauder Foundation, A. Alfred Taubman,
anonymous donor, and purchase.

16. *Flag.* 1958.
Encaustic on canvas,
41¼ × 60¾ in. (105 × 154 cm).
Jean-Christophe Castelli Collection, New York.

15

16

17. *Coat Hanger*. 1958.
    Crayon on paper,
    24½ × 21⅝ in. (62 × 54.5 cm).
    Mr. and Mrs. William Easton Collection.

18. *Tennyson*. 1959.
    Pastel on paper,
    30³⁄₁₆ × 21¾ in. (76.6 × 55.2 cm).
    Hirshhorn Museum and Sculpture Garden, Washington D.C.
    Gift of Joseph H. Hirshhorn, 1966.

17

18

19. *Figure 0.* 1959.
   Encaustic on canvas,
   20¼ × 15⅛ in. (51.5 × 38.5 cm).
   Private collection.

20. *Two Flags.* 1959.
   Plastic paint on canvas,
   79¼ × 58¼ in. (201 × 148 cm).
   Private collection.

19

20

21. *0 - 9.* 1959-1962.
    Plastic paint on canvas,
    20½ × 35½ in. (52 × 90 cm).
    Anne and Martin Z. Margulies Collection, Miami, Fla.

22. *0 - 9.* 1959.
    Encaustic and collage on canvas,
    20⅛ × 35 in. (51 × 89 cm).
    Ludwig Collection.

21

22

23. *False Start*. 1959.
Oil on canvas,
67¼ × 54 in. (171 × 137 cm).
Mr. and Mrs. S. I. Newhouse, Jr. Collection, New York.

24. *Shade*. 1959.
Encaustic on canvas with objects,
52 × 39 in. (132.1 × 99.1 cm).
Neue Galerie, Aachen.
Ludwig Collection.

25. *Jubilee*. 1960.
Pencil and graphite wash on paper,
28 × 21 in. (71.1 × 53.3 cm).
The Museum of Modern Art, New York.
The Joan Lester Avnet Collection.

24

25

26. *Painting with Two Balls.* 1960.
    Encaustic and collage on canvas with objects,
    65 × 54 in. (165 × 137 cm).
    The artist's collection.

27. *Study for Painting with Two Balls.* 1960.
Charcoal on paper,
24³⁄₈ × 18¹¹⁄₁₆ in. (61.9 × 47.4 cm).
Hirshhorn Museum and Sculpture Garden, Washington D.C.
Gift of Joseph H. Hirshhorn, 1966.

28. *Two Flags.* 1960.
Pencil and graphite wash on paper,
29¹⁄₂ × 21³⁄₄ in. (75 × 55 cm).
The artist's collection.

27

28

29. *Painted Bronze.* 1960.
Painted bronze,
5½ × 8 × 4¾ in. (14 × 20.3 × 12.1 cm).
Oeffentliche Kunstsammlung Basel, Kunstmuseum.
Ludwig-St Alban Collection.

30. *Night Driver.* 1960.
Chalk, pastel and pasted paper,
45 × 37 in. (114.3 × 94 cm).
Robert and Jane Meyerhoff Collection, Phoenix, Md.

31. *Target.* 1960.
Graphite wash on paper,
13½ × 13½ in. (34.3 × 34.3 cm).
Allen Memorial Art Museum, Oberlin College (Ohio).
Ruth C. Roush Fund for Contemporary Art.

29

30

31

32. *Zero Through Nine.* 1961.
    Oil on canvas,
    54 × 41¼ in. (137 × 104.5 cm).
    Private collection, Connecticut.

33. *0 Through 9.* 1961.
    Oil and charcoal on canvas,
    54⅛ × 41⅜ in. (137.3 × 104.9 cm).
    Hirshhorn Museum and Sculpture Garden,
    Washington D.C.

32

34. *Map.* 1961.
Oil on canvas,
78 × 123⅛ in. (198.2 × 314.7 cm).
The Museum of Modern Art, New York.
Gift of Mr. and Mrs. Robert R. Scull, 1963.

34

35. *Disppearance II*. 1961.
Encaustic and collage on canvas,
40 × 40 in. (101.6 × 101.6 cm).
The Museum of Modern Art, Toyama City, Japan.

36. *0 Through 9.* 1961.
   Sculpmetal relief,
   27×21 in. (68.5×53.3 cm).
   Edition: 4 ex.
   The artist's collection.

37. *M.* 1962.
   Oil on canvas with objects,
   36×24 in. (91.5×61 cm).
   The Seibu Museum of Art, Tokyo.

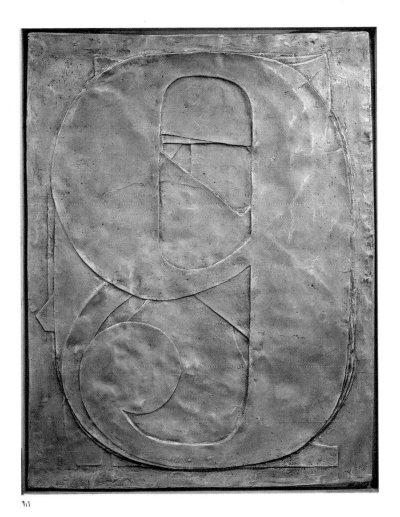

38. *Slow Field*. 1962.
Oil on canvas with objects,
71¼ × 35½ in. (181 × 90 cm).
Moderna Museet, Stockholm.

38

39. *Zone.* 1962.
Oil, encaustic and collage on canvas with objects,
60¼ × 36 in. (153 × 91.5 cm).
Kunsthaus, Zürich.

40

40. *Figure 2.* 1962.
Encaustic and collage on canvas,
51½ × 41½ in. (130.5 × 105.5 cm).
Oeffentliche Kunstsammlung Basel, Kunstmuseum.

41. *Alphabets.* 1962.
Oil on paper over canvas,
34 × 24 in. (86.3 × 61 cm).

42. *Device.* 1961-1962.
Oil on canvas with objects,
72 × 48⅛ × 4½ in. (183 × 122.3 × 11.4 cm).
Dallas Museum of Fine Arts.
Acquired in honor of Mrs. Eugene McDermott.
Dallas Art Museum League, Mr. and Mrs. George
V. Charlton, Mr. and Mrs. James B. Francis, Dr. and
Mrs. Ralph Greenlee, Jr., Mr. and Mrs. James H. W. Jacks,
Mr. and Mrs. Irvin W. Levy, Mrs. John W. O'Boyle,
Dr. Joanne Stroud.

41

42

43. *Diver*. 1962.
   Oil on canvas with objects,
   90 × 170 in. (228.5 × 432 cm), 5 panels.
   Irina and Norman Braman Collection.

44. *Land's End.* 1963.
     Oil on canvas with stick,
     67×48¼ in. (170.2×122.5 cm).
     San Francisco Museum of Modern Art.
     Gift of Mr. and Mrs. Harry W. Anderson.

45. *Diver.* 1963.
     Charcoal and pastel on paper,
     86½×71 in. (220×180.3 cm).
     Mrs. Victor W. Ganz Collection.

46. *Map.* 1963.
Encaustic and collage on canvas,
60 × 93 in. (152.5 × 236 cm).
Private collection.

47. *Field Painting.* 1963-1964.
Oil on canvas with objects,
72 × 36¾ in. (183 × 93 cm).
The artist's collection.

46

48. *According to What*. 1964.
   Oil on canvas with objets,
   88 × 192 in. (223.5 × 487.5 cm).
   Mr. and Mrs. S. I. Newhouse, Jr. Collection, New York.

49. *Untitled*. 1964-1965.
   Oil on canvas with objects,
   72 × 168 in. (183 × 426.5 cm).
   Stedelijk Museum, Amsterdam.

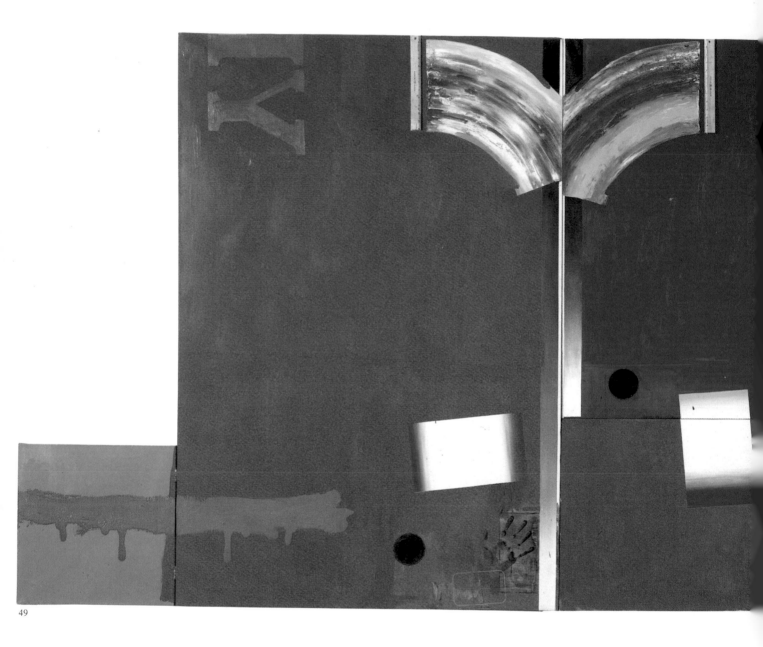

49

50. *Eddingsville.* 1965.
   Oil on canvas with objects,
   68 × 122½ in. (172.5 × 311 cm).
   Museum Ludwig, Cologne.

51. *Flag.* 1960-1966
   Encaustic on paper over canvas.
   17½ × 26¾ in. (44.5 × 68 cm).
   Michael Crichton Collection.

50

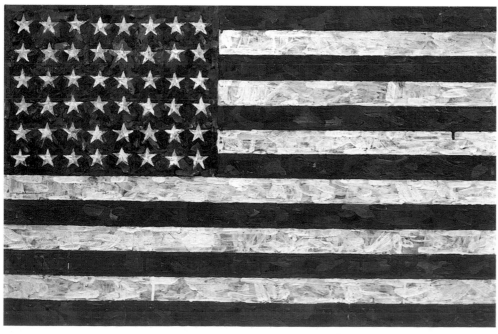

51

52. *Studio 2.* 1966.
    Oil on canvas,
    70 × 125 in. (178 × 317.5 cm).
    Victor W. Ganz Collection.

53. *Three Flags. c.* 1959-1966.
    Pencil on paper,
    14½ × 20 in. (36.9 × 50.8 cm).
    Victoria and Albert Museum, London.

52

53

54. *Target*. 1967-1969.
   Oil and collage on canvas,
   61½ × 61½ in. (156 × 156 cm).
   Private collection.

54

55. *Numbers.* 1966.
    Pencil, brush and ink on brown paper,
    26 × 21⅝ in. (76 × 54.9 cm).
    The Museum of Modern Art, New York.
    Gift of Mrs. Bliss Parkinson in honor of René d'Harnoncourt.

56. Drawing for *O'Hara: In Memory of My Feelings.* 1967.
    Pencil and graphite wash on plastic,
    12⅝ × 19 in. (32 × 48.2 cm).
    The Museum of Modern Art, New York.
    Gift of the artist.

55

56

57. *Harlem Light*. 1967.
Oil on canvas with collage,
78 × 172 in. (198 × 437 cm).
David Whitney Collection.

57

58. *Wall Piece*. 1968.
Oil on canvas with collage,
72 × 110¼ in. (183 × 280 cm).
The artist's collection.

59. *Screen Piece 4*. 1968.
    Oil on canvas,
    50¾ × 34 in. (129 × 86.3 cm).
    Robert and Jane Meyerhoff Collection, Phoenix, Md.

60. *The Critic Smiles*. 1969.
    Lead relief with tin leaf and cast gold,
    23 × 17 in. (58.4 × 43.2 cm).
    Edition: 60 ex.
    The artist's collection.

61. *Map* (Based on Buckminster Fuller's Dymaxion
    Airocean World). 1966-1971.
    Encaustic and collage on canvas,
    186×396 in. (472×1005 cm).
    Museum Ludwig, Cologne.

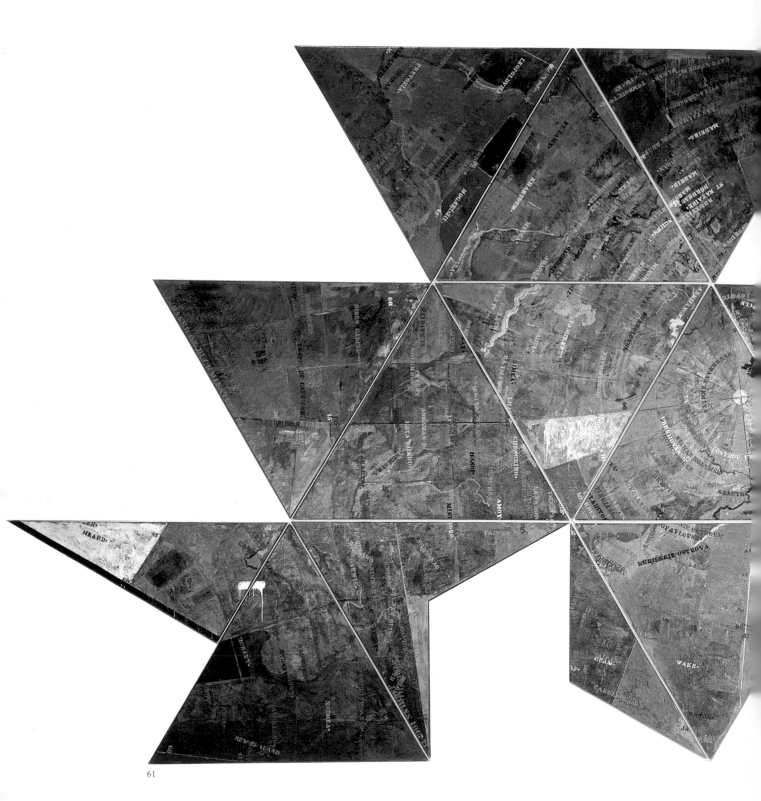

61

62. *Voice II*. 1971.
    Oil and collage on canvas,
    3 panels, each 72 × 50 in. (183 × 127 cm).
    Oeffentliche Kunstsammlung Basel, Kunstmuseum.

63. *Untitled I*. 1969.
    Pencil and charcoal, on white wove paper,
    27¾ × 33⅝ in. (70.5 × 85.4 cm).
    The Art Institute of Chicago.
    Gift of the Society of Contemporary American Art.

64. *Voice*. 1969.
    Brush and graphite wash,
    36¼ × 27½ in. (92 × 69.8 cm).
    The Museum of Modern Art, New York. Purchase.

65. Study for *According to What*. 1969.
    Pencil and brush and tempera,
    34¾ × 26 in. (88.3 × 66.1 cm).
    The Baltimore Museum of Art.
    Thomas E. Benesch Memorial Collection.

62

63

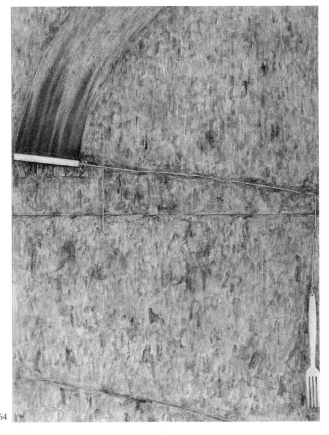

64

65

66. *Untitled.* 1972.
   Oil, encaustic and collage on canvas with objects,
   72 × 192 in. (183 × 487.5 cm).
   Museum Ludwig, Cologne.

66

67. *Decoy.* 1971.
Oil on canvas with brass grummet,
47×29½ in. (119×75 cm).
Mrs. Victor W. Ganz Collection.

68. *Ale Cans V.* 1975.
India ink on (folded) paper,
18×22¼ in. (45.7×56.5 cm).
The John and Mable Ringling Museum of
Art: Purchased with matching funds from
The National Endowment for the Arts,
Mrs. William Cox and Mr. and Mrs.
A. Werk Cook.

67

68

69. *Target.* 1974.
   Encaustic and collage on canvas,
   61¼ × 53¼ in. (155.5 × 135.5 cm).
   The Seibu Museum of Art, Tokyo.

70

70. *Scent*. 1974.
Encaustic and collage on canvas,
72 × 126 in. (183 × 320 cm).
Neue Galerie, Aachen.
Ludwig Collection.

71. *Weeping Women.* 1975.
Encaustic and collage on canvas,
50 × 102¼ in. (127 × 260 cm).
Mr. and Mrs. S. I. Newhouse, Jr. Collection, New York.

72. *The Barber's Tree.* 1975.
Encaustic on canvas,
34¼ × 54½ in. (87 × 138 cm).
Neue Galerie, Aachen.
Ludwig Collection.

73. *Usuyuki.* 1977-1978.
Encaustic and collage on canvas,
3 panels, 35⅛ × 56⅝ in. (89 × 143.5 cm).
The artist's collection.

71

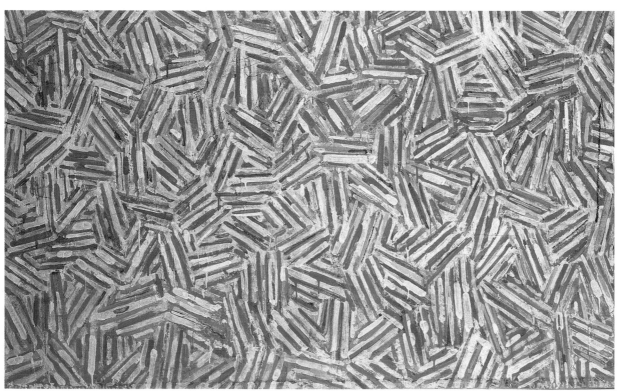

72

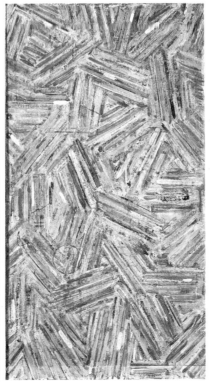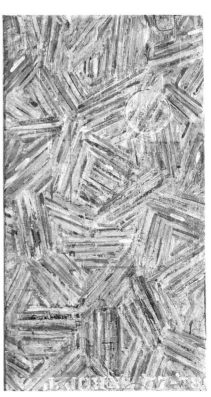

74. *End Paper*. 1976.
 Oil on canvas,
 2 panels, 60×69½ in. (152.5×176.5 cm).
 Davis Whitney Collection.

75. *Usuyuki*. 1977-1978.
 Encaustic and collage on canvas,
 56¾×18 in. (144×45.7 cm).
 Private collection.

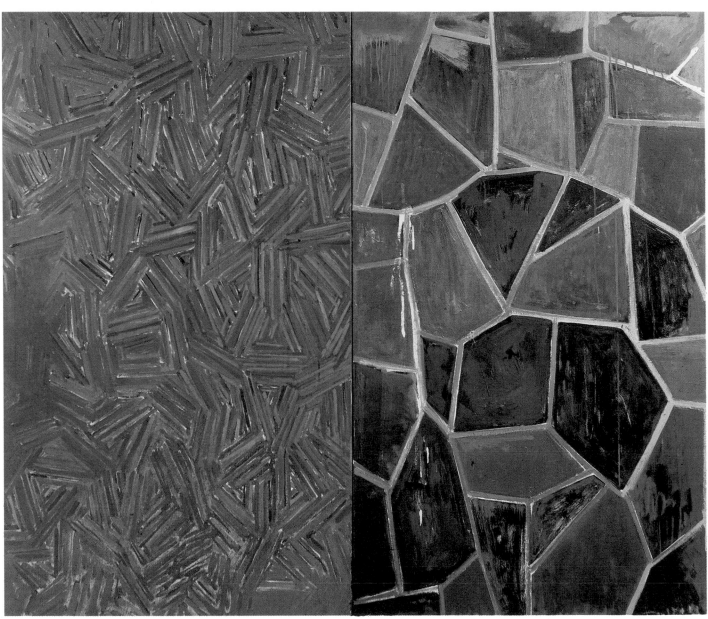

74

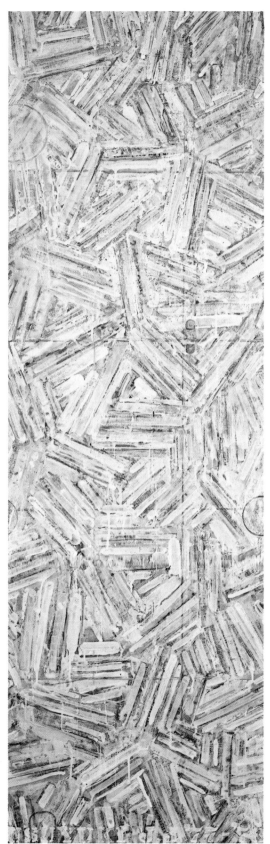

75

76. *Two Flags*. 1973-1977.
Oil on paper over canvas,
53⅞ × 71⅝ in. (136.4 × 181.5 cm).
Private collection.

77. *Numbers.* 1963-1978.
    Aluminiun relief,
    57½×43½ in. (146×110.5 cm).
    The artist's collection.

78. *Savarin.* 1977.
    Brush, pen and ink,
    36¼×26⅛ in. (92.1×66.4 cm).
    The Museum of Modern Art, New York.
    Gift of the Lauder Foundation, Inc.

77

78

79

80

79. *Untitled.* 1980.
    Acrylic on plastic over canvas,
    $30^{3}/_{8} \times 54^{3}/_{8}$ in. (77 × 138 cm).
    Gagosian Gallery, New York.

80. *Untitled.* 1980.
    Oil on canvas,
    30 × 54 in. (76.2 × 137 cm).
    The artist's collection.

81. *Untitled.* 1980.
    Encaustic and collage on canvas,
    30 × 54 in. (76.2 × 137 cm).
    Raymond Nasher Collection, Dallas.

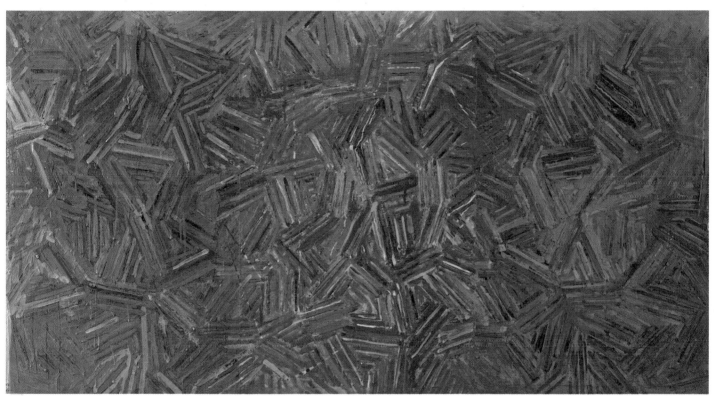

81

82. *Tantric Detail I.* 1980.
    Oil on canvas,
    50⅛ × 34⅛ in. (127.3 × 86.5 cm).
    The artist's collection.

83. *Tantric Detail II.* 1981.
    Oil on canvas,
    $50\frac{1}{8} \times 34\frac{1}{8}$ in. (127.3 × 86.5 cm).
    The artist's collection.

84. *Tantric Detail III*. 1981.
    Oil on canvas,
    50⅛ × 34⅛ in. (127.3 × 86.5 cm).
    The artist's collection.

85. *In the Studio*. 1982.
    Encaustic on canvas with objects,
    72 × 48 × 4 in. (183 × 122 × 10 cm).
    The artist's collection.

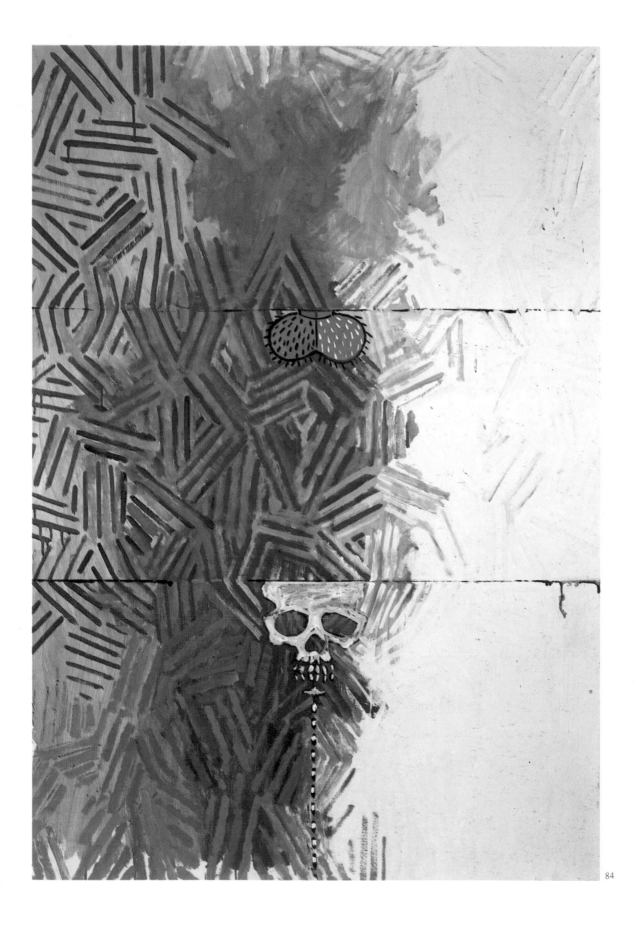

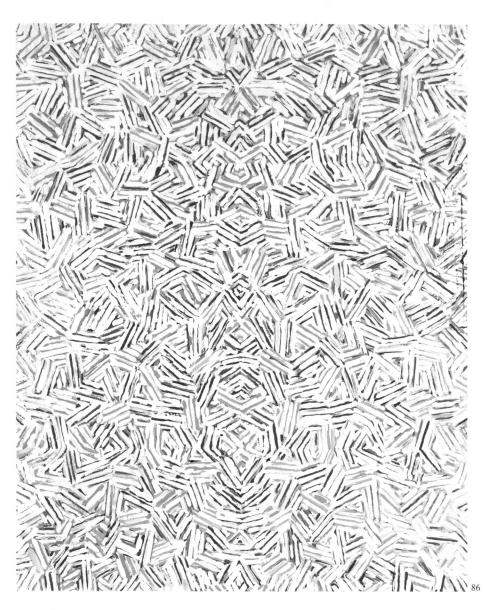

86

86. *Dancers on a Plane*. 1982.
Oil on canvas,
29⅞ × 23¾ in. (76 × 60 cm).
The artist's collection.

87. *Untitled*. 1983.
Ink on plastic,
24¾ × 36¼ in. (63 × 92.1 cm).
The Museum of Modern Art, New York
Gift of the Lauder Foundation, Inc.

88. *Between the Clock and the Bed*. 1981.
Oil on canvas, three panels,
72 × 126¼ in. (183 × 321 cm).
The artist's collection.

89. *Between the Clock and the Bed*. 1981.
Encaustic on canvas, three panels,
72 × 126¼ in. (183 × 321 cm).
The Museum of Modern Art, New York.
Gift of Agnes Gund.

90. *Between the Clock and the Bed*. 1982-1983.
Encaustic on canvas, three panels,
72 × 126⅛ in. (183 × 320 cm).
Virginia Museum of Fine Arts, Richmond.
Gift of Sydney and Frances Lewis
Foundation.

87

88

89

90

91. *Ventriloquist.* 1983.
Encaustic on canvas,
75 × 50 in. (190.5 × 127 cm).
The Museum of Fine Arts, Houston.
Purchase: Agnes Cullen Endowment Fund.

92. *Untitled.* 1984.
Encaustic on canvas,
50 × 34 in. (127 × 86.3 cm).
Larry Gagosian Collection, New York.

93. *Untitled*. 1984.
    Oil on canvas,
    75 × 50 in. (190.5 × 127 cm).
    Private collection.

94. *Untitled*. 1984.
    Encaustic on canvas,
    50 × 34 in. (127 × 86.3 cm).
    The artist's collection.

95. *Untitled*. 1984.
    Encaustic on canvas,
    50 × 75 in. (127 × 190.5 cm).
    The artist's collection.

94

95

96. *Racing Thoughts.* 1984.
   Oil on canvas,
   50 × 75 in. (127 × 190.5 cm).
   Robert and Jane Meyerhoff Collection, Phoenix, Md.

97. *Spring.* 1986.
   Encaustic on canvas,
   75 × 50 in. (190.5 × 127 cm).
   Mr. and Mrs. S. I. Newhouse, Jr. Collection, New York.

96

98. *Summer*. 1985.
Encaustic on canvas,
75 × 50 in. (190.5 × 127 cm).
Philip Johnson Collection.

99. *Fall.* 1986.
Encaustic on canvas,
75 × 50 in. (190.5 × 127 cm).
The artist's collection.

100. *Winter.* 1986.
    Encaustic on canvas,
    75 × 50 in. (190.5 × 127 cm).
    Mr. and Mrs. Asher B. Edelman Collection, New York.

101. *Untitled.* 1986.
    Oil on canvas,
    17³⁄₈ × 11³⁄₄ in. (44 × 29.5 cm).
    The artist's collection.

102. *Untitled.* 1986-1987.
    Oil on canvas,
    32 × 25⁵⁄₈ in. (81.2 × 65 cm).
    The artist's collection.

101

102

103. *Flags.* 1986.
Oil on canvas,
25½ × 33 in. (64.5 × 84 cm).
Emily Fisher Landau Collection.

104. *Untitled.* 1987.
Encaustic and collage on canvas,
50 × 75 in. (127 × 190.5 cm).
Robert and Jane Meyerhoff Collection, Phoenix, Md.

103

104

105. *Two Flags on Orange.* 1986-1987.
Acrylic, ink and crayon on mylar,
34×24 in. (86.3×61 cm).
Edward J. Minskoff Collection, New York.

106. *Untitled.* 1987.
Encaustic on canvas,
50×75 in. (127×190.5 cm).
Hirshhorn Museum and Sculpture Garden,
Washington D.C.

105

106

107. *A Souvenir for Andrew Monk.* 1987.
Chalk, charcoal, graphite and collage on paper,
42 × 28 in. (106.5 × 71 cm).
The artist's collection.

108. *Untitled.* 1988.
Encaustic on canvas,
48¼ × 60¼ in. (122.5 × 153 cm).
Anne and Joel Ehren Kranz Collection.

107

108

GRAPHIC WORK

109

111

110

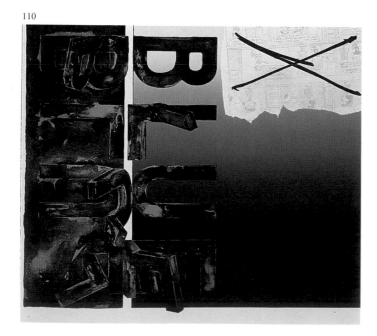

109. *Figure 1.* 1969.
   From the series "Color Numeral."
   Color lithograph, 38 × 31 in. (96.5 × 78.7 cm).
   Edition: 40 ex. Publisher: Gemini G.E.L., Los Angeles.

110. *Fragments - According to What - Bent "Blue."* 1971.
   Color lithograph with transfer,
   second State, 25½ × 28¾ in. (64.8 × 73 cm).
   Edition: 66 ex. Publisher: Gemini G.E.L., Los Angeles.

111. *Four Panels from "Untitled."* 1973-1974.
   Color lithograph with embossing on four sheets,
   each 40 × 29¾ in. (101.6 × 75.4 cm).
   Edition: 45 ex. Publisher: Gemini G.E.L., Los Angeles.

112. *HandFootSockFloor.* 1974.
   From the series "Casts from Untitled."
   Color lithograph, 30¾ × 22¾ in. (78.1 × 57.8 cm).
   Edition: 48 ex. Publisher: Gemini G.E.L., Los Angeles.

113. *N.º 6.* 1976.
   From the series "Untitled 1975", 6 lithographs.
   Color lithograph, 30 × 30 in. (76.5 × 76.5 cm).
   Edition: 60 ex. Publisher: Gemini G.E.L., Los Angeles.

112

113

114. *Untitled (Red, Yellow, Blue)*. 1982.
Three color etchings, each 42¼×29½ in. (107×75 cm).
Edition: 77 ex. Publisher: Petersburg Press Inc., New York.

115. *Land's End*. 1978.
Color etching, 41¾×29½ in. (106×75 cm).
Edition: 56 ex. Publisher: Petersburg Press Inc., New York.

116. *Periscope I*. 1979.
Color lithograph, 50×36¼ in. (127×92 cm).
Edition: 65 ex. Publisher: Gemini G.E.L., Los Angeles.

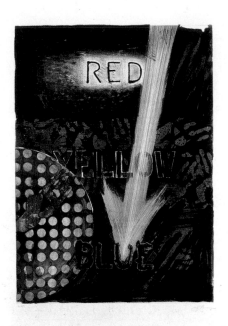 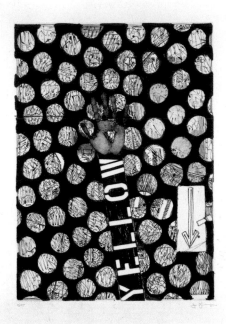 

114

115

116

117. *Target with Plaster Casts.* 1978-1980.
Etching and aquatint in color,
29½ × 22¼ in. (75.1 × 56.7 cm).
Edition: 88 ex.
Publisher: Petersburg Press Inc., New York.

118. *Untitled.* 1977-1980.
Color lithograph,
34¼ × 30¼ in. (87 × 76.8 cm).
Edition: 60 ex.
Publisher: Gemini G.E.L., Los Angeles.

119. *Periscope.* 1978-1981.
Color etching,
41¼ × 29½ in. (105 × 75 cm).
Edition: 88 ex.
Publisher: Petersburg Press Inc., New York.

120. *Untitled.* 1981.
Color etching from 3 plates,
16¼ × 13 in. (41 × 33 cm).
Edition: 78 ex.
Publisher: Petersburg Press Inc., New York.

117

118

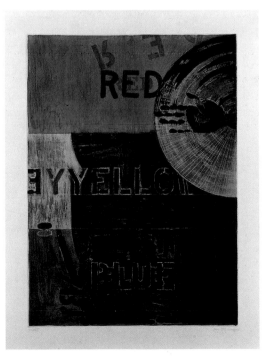

119

120

TABLE OF ILLUSTRATIONS

42. *Device.* 1961-1962.
Oil on canvas with objects,
72 × 48⅛ × 4½ in. (183 × 122.3 × 11.4 cm).
Dallas Museum of Fine Arts. Acquired
in honor of Mrs. Eugene McDermott.
Dallas Art Museum League, Mr. and
Mrs. George V. Charlton, Mr. and
Mrs. James B. Francis, Dr. and Mrs.
Ralph Greenlee, Jr., Mr. and Mrs.
James H. W. Jacks, Mr. and Mrs. Irvin
W. Levy, Mrs. John W. O'Boyle, Dr.
Joanne Stroud.

43. *Diver.* 1962.
Oil on canvas with objects,
90 × 170 in. (228.5 × 432 cm), 5 panels.
Irina and Norman Braman Collection.

44. *Land's End.* 1963.
Oil on canvas with stick,
67 × 48¼ in. (170.2 × 122.5 cm).
San Francisco Museum of Modern Art.
Gift of Mr. and Mrs. Harry W.
Anderson.

45. *Diver.* 1963.
Charcoal and pastel on paper,
86½ × 71 in. (220 × 180.3 cm).
Mrs. Victor W. Ganz Collection.

46. *Map.* 1963.
Encaustic and collage on canvas,
60 × 93 in. (152.5 × 236 cm).
Private collection.

47. *Field Painting.* 1963-1964.
Oil on canvas with objects,
72 × 36¾ in. (183 × 93 cm).
The artist's collection.

48. *According to What.* 1964.
Oil on canvas with objets,
88 × 192 in. (223.5 × 487.5 cm).
Mr. and Mrs. S. I. Newhouse, Jr.
Collection, New York.

49. *Untitled.* 1964-1965.
Oil on canvas with objects,
72 × 168 in. (183 × 426.5 cm).
Stedelijk Museum, Amsterdam.

50. *Eddingsville.* 1965.
Oil on canvas with objects,
68 × 122½ in. (172.5 × 311 cm).
Museum Ludwig, Cologne.

51. *Flag.* 1960-1966.
Encaustic on paper over canvas.
17½ × 26¾ in. (44.5 × 68 cm).
Michael Crichton Collection.

52. *Studio 2.* 1966.
Oil on canvas,
70 × 125 in. (178 × 317.5 cm).
Victor W. Ganz Collection.

53. *Three Flags. c.* 1959-1966.
Pencil on paper,
14½ × 20 in. (36.9 × 50.8 cm).
Victoria and Albert Museum, London.

54. *Target.* 1967-1969.
Oil and collage on canvas,
61½ × 61½ in. (156 × 156 cm).
Private collection.

55. *Numbers.* 1966.
Pencil, brush and ink on brown paper,
26 × 21⅝ in. (76 × 54.9 cm).
The Museum of Modern Art,
New York. Gift of Mrs. Bliss
Parkinson in honor of René
d'Harnoncourt.

56. Drawing for *O'Hara: In Memory of
My Feelings.* 1967.
Pencil and graphite wash on plastic,
12⅝ × 19 in. (32 × 48.2 cm).
The Museum of Modern Art,
New York. Gift of the artist.

57. *Harlem Light.* 1967.
Oil on canvas with collage,
78 × 172 in. (198 × 437 cm).
David Whitney Collection.

58. *Wall Piece.* 1968.
Oil on canvas with collage,
72 × 110¼ in. (183 × 280 cm).
The artist's collection.

59. *Screen Piece 4.* 1968.
Oil on canvas,
50¾ × 34 in. (129 × 86.3 cm).
Robert and Jane Meyerhoff Collection,
Phoenix, Md.

60. *The Critic Smiles.* 1969.
Lead relief with tin leaf and cast gold,
23 × 17 in. (58.4 × 43.2 cm).
Edition: 60 ex.
The artist's collection.

61. *Map* (Based on Buckminster Fuller's
Dymaxion Airocean World). 1966-1971.
Encaustic and collage on canvas,
186 × 396 in. (472 × 1005 cm).
Museum Ludwig, Cologne.

62. *Voice II.* 1971.
Oil and collage on canvas,
3 panels, each 72 × 50 in. (183 × 127 cm).
Oeffentliche Kunstsammlung Basel,
Kunstmuseum.

63. *Untitled I.* 1969.
Pencil and charcoal, on white wove
paper, 27¾ × 33⅝ in. (70.5 × 85.4 cm).
The Art Institute of Chicago.
Gift of the Society of Contemporary
American Art.

64. *Voice.* 1969.
Brush and graphite wash,
36¼ × 27½ in. (92 × 69.8 cm).
The Museum of Modern Art,
New York. Purchase.

65. Study for *According to What.* 1969.
Pencil and brush and tempera,
34¾ × 26 in. (88.3 × 66.1 cm).
The Baltimore Museum of Art.
Thomas E. Benesch Memorial
Collection.

66. *Untitled.* 1972.
Oil, encaustic and collage on canvas
with objects,
72 × 192 in. (183 × 487.5 cm).
Museum Ludwig, Cologne.

67. *Decoy.* 1971.
Oil on canvas with brass grummet,
47 × 29½ in. (119 × 75 cm).
Mrs. Victor W. Ganz Collection.

68. *Ale Cans V.* 1975.
India ink on (folded) paper,
18 × 22¼ in. (45.7 × 56.5 cm).
The John and Mable Ringling Museum
of Art: Purchased with matching funds
from The National Endowment for the
Arts, Mrs. William Cox and Mr. and
Mrs. A. Werk Cook.

69. *Target.* 1974.
Encaustic and collage on canvas,
61¼ × 53¼ in. (155.5 × 135.5 cm).
The Seibu Museum of Art, Tokyo.

70. *Scent.* 1974.
Encaustic and collage on canvas,
72 × 126 in. (183 × 320 cm).
Neue Galerie, Aachen. Ludwig
Collection.

71. *Weeping Women.* 1975.
Encaustic and collage on canvas,
50 × 102¼ in. (127 × 260 cm).
Mr. and Mrs. S. I. Newhouse, Jr.
Collection, New York.

72. *The Barber's Tree.* 1975.
Encaustic on canvas,
34¼ × 54½ in. (87 × 138 cm).
Neue Galerie, Aachen. Ludwig
Collection.

73. *Usuyuki.* 1977-1978.
Encaustic and collage on canvas,
3 panels, 35⅛ × 56⅝ in. (89 × 143.5 cm).
The artist's collection.

74. *End Paper.* 1976.
Oil on canvas,
2 panels, 60 × 69½ in. (152.5 × 176.5 cm).
Davis Whitney Collection.

75. *Usuyuki.* 1977-1978.
Encaustic and collage on canvas,
56¾ × 18 in. (144 × 45.7 cm).
Private collection.

76. *Two Flags.* 1973-1977.
Oil on paper over canvas,
53⅞ × 71⅝ in. (136.4 × 181.5 cm).
Private collection.

77. *Numbers.* 1963-1978.
Aluminiun relief,
57½ × 43½ in. (146 × 110.5 cm).
The artist's collection.

78. *Savarin.* 1977.
Brush, pen and ink,
36¼ × 26⅛ in. (92.1 × 66.4 cm).
The Museum of Modern Art,
New York. Gift of the Lauder
Foundation, Inc.

79. *Untitled.* 1980.
Acrylic on plastic over canvas,
30⅜ × 54⅜ in. (77 × 138 cm).
Gagosian Gallery, New York.

80. *Untitled.* 1980.
Oil on canvas,
30 × 54 in. (76.2 × 137 cm).
The artist's collection.

81. *Untitled.* 1980.
Encaustic and collage on canvas,
30 × 54 in. (76.2 × 137 cm).
Raymond Nasher Collection, Dallas.

82. *Tantric Detail I.* 1980.
Oil on canvas,
50⅛ × 34⅛ in. (127.3 × 86.5 cm).
The artist's collection.

83. *Tantric Detail II.* 1981.
Oil on canvas,
50⅛ × 34⅛ in. (127.3 × 86.5 cm).
The artist's collection.

84. *Tantric Detail III.* 1981.
Oil on canvas,
50⅛ × 34⅛ in. (127.3 × 86.5 cm).
The artist's collection.

85. *In the Studio.* 1982.
Encaustic on canvas with objects,
72 × 48 × 4 in. (183 × 122 × 10 cm).
The artist's collection.

86. *Dancers on a Plane.* 1982.
Oil on canvas,
29⅞ × 23¾ in. (76 × 60 cm).
The artist's collection.

87. *Untitled.* 1983.
Ink on plastic,
24¾ × 36¼ in. (63 × 92.1 cm).
The Museum of Modern Art,
New York. Gift of the Lauder
Foundation, Inc.

88. *Between the Clock and the Bed.* 1981.
Oil on canvas, three panels,
72 × 126¼ in. (183 × 321 cm).
The artist's collection.

89. *Between the Clock and the Bed.* 1981.
Encaustic on canvas, three panels,
72 × 126¼ in. (183 × 321 cm).
The Museum of Modern Art,
New York. Gift of Agnes Gund.

90. *Between the Clock and the Bed.*
1982-1983.
Encaustic on canvas, three panels,
72 × 126⅛ in. (183 × 320 cm).
Virginia Museum of Fine Arts,
Richmond. Gift of Sydney and Frances
Lewis Foundation.

91. *Ventriloquist.* 1983.
Encaustic on canvas,
75 × 50 in. (190.5 × 127 cm).
The Museum of Fine Arts, Houston.
Purchase: Agnes Cullen Endowment
Fund.

92. *Untitled.* 1984.
Encaustic on canvas,
50 × 34 in. (127 × 86.3 cm).
Larry Gagosian Collection, New York.

93. *Untitled.* 1984.
Oil on canvas,
75 × 50 in. (190.5 × 127 cm).
Private collection.

94. *Untitled.* 1984.
Encaustic on canvas,
50 × 34 in. (127 × 86.3 cm).
The artist's collection.

95. *Untitled.* 1984.
Encaustic on canvas,
50 × 75 in. (127 × 190.5 cm).
The artist's collection.

96. *Racing Thoughts.* 1984.
Oil on canvas,
50 × 75 in. (127 × 190.5 cm).
Robert and Jane Meyerhoff Collection,
Phoenix, Md.

97. *Spring.* 1986.
Encaustic on canvas,
75 × 50 in. (190.5 × 127 cm).
Mr. and Mrs. S. I. Newhouse, Jr.
Collection, New York.

98. *Summer.* 1985.
Encaustic on canvas,
75 × 50 in. (190.5 × 127 cm).
Philip Johnson Collection.

99. *Fall.* 1986.
Encaustic on canvas,
75 × 50 in. (190.5 × 127 cm).
The artist's collection.

100. *Winter.* 1986.
Encaustic on canvas,
75 × 50 in. (190.5 × 127 cm).
Mr. and Mrs. Asher B. Edelman
Collection, New York.

101. *Untitled.* 1986.
Oil on canvas,
17⅜ × 11¾ in. (44 × 29.5 cm).
The artist's collection.

102. *Untitled.* 1986-1987.
Oil on canvas,
32 × 25⅝ in. (81.2 × 65 cm).
The artist's collection.

103. *Flags.* 1986.
Oil on canvas,
25½ × 33 in. (64.5 × 84 cm).
Emily Fisher Landau Collection.

104. *Untitled.* 1987.
Encaustic and collage on canvas,
50 × 75 in. (127 × 190.5 cm).
Robert and Jane Meyerhoff
Collection, Phoenix, Md.

105. *Two Flags on Orange.* 1986-1987.
Acrylic, ink and crayon on mylar,
34 × 24 in. (86.3 × 61 cm).
Edward J. Minskoff Collection,
New York.

106. *Untitled.* 1987.
Encaustic on canvas,
50 × 75 in. (127 × 190.5 cm).
Hirshhorn Museum and Sculpture
Garden, Washington D.C.

107. *A Souvenir for Andrew Monk.* 1987.
Chalk, charcoal, graphite and collage
on paper, 42 × 28 in. (106.5 × 71 cm).
The artist's collection.

108. *Untitled.* 1988.
Encaustic on canvas,
48¼ × 60¼ in. (122.5 × 153 cm).
Anne and Joel Ehren Kranz
Collection.

GRAPHIC WORK

109. *Figure 1.* 1969.
From the series "Color Numeral."
Color lithograph, 38 × 31 in.
(96.5 × 78.7 cm).
Edition: 40 ex.
Publisher: Gemini G.E.L.,
Los Angeles.

110. *Fragments - According to What - Bent
"Blue."* 1971.
Color lithograph with transfer,
second State, 25½ × 28¾ in.
(64.8 × 73 cm).
Edition: 66 ex.
Publisher: Gemini G.E.L.,
Los Angeles.

111. *Four Panels from "Untitled."*
1973-1974.
Color lithograph with embossing on
four sheets, each 40 × 29¾ in.
(101.6 × 75.4 cm).
Edition: 45 ex.
Publisher: Gemini G.E.L.,
Los Angeles.

112. *HandFootSockFloor.* 1974.
From the series "Casts from
Untitled." Color lithograph,
30¾ × 22¾ in. (78.1 × 57.8 cm).
Edition: 48 ex.
Publisher: Gemini G.E.L.,
Los Angeles.

113. *N.° 6.* 1976.
From the series "Untitled 1975", 6
lithographs. Color lithograph,
30 × 30 in. (76.5 × 76.5 cm).
Edition: 60 ex.
Publisher: Gemini G.E.L.,
Los Angeles.

114. *Untitled (Red, Yellow, Blue).* 1982.
Three color etchings, each
42¼ × 29½ in. (107 × 75 cm).
Edition: 77 ex.
Publisher: Petersburg Press Inc.,
New York.

115. *Land's End.* 1978.
Color etching, 41¾ × 29½ in.
(106 × 75 cm).
Edition: 56 ex.
Publisher: Petersburg Press Inc.,
New York.

116. *Periscope I.* 1979.
Color lithograph, 50 × 36¼ in.
(127 × 92 cm).
Edition: 65 ex.
Publisher: Gemini G.E.L.,
Los Angeles.

117. *Target with Plaster Casts.* 1978-1980.
Etching and aquatint in color,
29½ × 22¼ in. (75.1 × 56.7 cm).
Edition: 88 ex.
Publisher: Petersburg Press Inc.,
New York.

118. *Untitled.* 1977-1980.
Color lithograph,
34¼ × 30¼ in. (87 × 76.8 cm).
Edition: 60 ex.
Publisher: Gemini G.E.L.,
Los Angeles.

119. *Periscope.* 1978-1981.
Color etching,
41¼ × 29½ in. (105 × 75 cm).
Edition: 88 ex.
Publisher: Petersburg Press Inc.,
New York.

120. *Untitled.* 1981.
Color etching from 3 plates,
16¼ × 13 in. (41 × 33 cm).
Edition: 78 ex.
Publisher: Petersburg Press Inc.,
New York.